Praise for
Writing In A Convertible With The Top Down

Wise and constructive. These letters shed light on writing as a process and let you feel you're sitting in on an intimate, empowering writers' group.

—Judith Applebaum, *How to Get Happily Published*

I used to think there could never be a book about writing as good as Natalie Goldberg's *Writing Down the Bones*. But *Writing in a Convertible* really is, as its subtitle says, *A Unique Guide for Writers*.

—Patricia Holt, *San Francisco Chronicle*

Writing

IN A CONVERTIBLE
WITH THE TOP DOWN

A Unique Guide for Writers

BY SHEILA BENDER &
CHRISTI KILLIEN GLOVER

Copyright © 2015 Sheila Bender and Christi Killien Glover

All rights reserved. No part of this publication may be reproduced, distributed, or transmitted in any form or by any means, including photocopying, recording, or other electronic or mechanical methods, without the prior written permission of the publisher, except in the case of brief quotations embodied in critical reviews and certain other noncommercial uses permitted by copyright law. For permission requests, write to the publisher, addressed "Attention: Permissions Coordinator," at the address below.

394 Colman Drive

Port Townsend WA 98361

Printed in the United States of America

ISBN 978-1-943224-01-2

Summary: A fun and practical guide to writing that will help your writing process be as breezy as driving in a convertible on a summer's day. The authors' prompts and personal insights will shift you into creative gear so you can speed successfully on your way to authentic writing. Sheila Bender and Christi Killien Glover offer the right roadmaps for helping you become the writer you know you can be. It's time to go for the green lights in your writing journey.

To my children Emily and Seth and my husband Kurt for their love and enthusiasm, and to all my teachers— which includes all of my students.

Sheila Bender

For the Killiens, Overturfs, Austins, Gillmans, and Glovers, all my families, whom I love and from whom I continue to learn.

Christi Killien Glover

Contents

Note: Each chapter is followed by two short sections summarizing its key point and suggesting writing exercises that apply the lesson.

introduction · · · 9

one · · · The Bus: How do we get started writing and keep going? · · · 15

two · · · Peonies: How do we continue our enthusiasm for writing day after day? · · · 25

three · · · Garbage: How do we overcome writer's block? · · · 29

four · · · Molasses: Where does the meaning in a story come from? · · · 35

five · · · Beach House: How do writers get the conscious mind to meld with the unconscious? · · · 43

six · · · Cherry Trees: How do we use other people's writing to help ourselves write? · · · 55

seven	The Bridge on the River Kwai: How does a writer visualize the structure of a story?	**63**
eight	Raspberry Picking: How can writers use readers' responses to refine their perceptions of their own writing?	**75**
nine	The Dentist: How do we create a good climate for story growing?	**83**
ten	Airports, Nursing Homes and Cafés: How do writers keep their writing from being boring?	**93**
eleven	Highway Patrol: How do we help each other as writing partners?	**105**
twelve	Porcupines: How do we defend our creative process in the face of resistance?	**123**
thirteen	Freshman: What is the writer's job?	**137**
fourteen	Garage Sales: Where does the writer discover treasures?	**147**

classic books for writers	**157**
notes on the authors	**165**

introduction

> "Suddenly you are sitting in your chair
> fascinated by your own mundane life."
> —Natalie Goldberg, *Writing Down the Bones*

From Christi Killien Glover

We were virtually strangers when we began the correspondence that makes up this book.

I had met Sheila at a fall conference for writers who spoke in the schools. Her table of materials was next to mine. She was short, brown-haired, and transplanted from the East Coast. All I knew about her then was that she wrote poems and plays and taught writing.

To Sheila, I was a taller, blonde-haired West Coast children's book writer who spoke at conferences a lot and was frustrated with how ill-run and repetitious so many of them were.

During that day, in bits and pieces, as people came and went from our tables, Sheila described her writing workshops to me. I told her how I wished I were home writing.

We liked each other well enough and exchanged phone numbers even though Sheila would be leaving soon for Berkeley, CA, where her husband would be spending some months on a computer job.

Almost a year later, when Sheila was back in town, and after I'd agreed to speak at several more conferences including a teacher's conference in Yakima that coming fall (Don't ask me why; I was scared to death to do it), I called her and asked her if she would be interested in writing a book with me about writing. This seems to be the way I work out problems—write a book about them.

Sheila was interested. (Unlike me, Sheila can work on five different projects at once.) But there was one snag. Kurt, her husband, was going to be working in Berkeley again, and she'd only be in town intermittently.

So we corresponded. Neither of us had written letters like this before. By that I mean letters about writing. In our letters, we taught each other our approaches to writing, our starting place with new work, and the ways we devised to continue working on our writing.

The letters ended up revealing our personal lives, as writing does. In some letters I was depressed, in others flying high. Sheila wrote to me from wherever she was, in cafes, in Texas, and on airplanes. I wrote from home and family excursions.

Writing In A Convertible With The Top Down

When Sheila returned to Seattle, we didn't know if we had a writing book, but we knew one another! And we both knew more about writing. Why not make the bulk of the book our correspondence?

It turned out that the letters have a special magic about them; they show how writing is not a linear process, how as writers we unconsciously fulfill a design as we write. Grouping the letters into the metaphors came later, after we hired our agent, Elizabeth Wales, who said the book needed chapters and shape.

Writing in a New Convertible is about writing. It's about what to pay attention to in our lives as writers. We learned that our lives reveal the writing process—whether we're sorting garbage, visiting dying relatives in nursing homes, or sitting at the kitchen table staring at a blossoming cherry tree.

We grouped our letters in the order that we wrote them, and for some of you, a straight-through read might work best. This way you get my story as I go through the process of writing a novel.

For others, reading appropriate sections might work better. That's why we've added the questions on the CONTENTS page. Sometimes you come to a writing book with a specific problem, like *Where does the meaning in the story come from? What is this story about, really?*

I still look back to the letters for comfort and encouragement. You will, too, and they will show you how to see metaphors about writing in your own lives. But most importantly, they will help you to write.

From Sheila Bender

Since the book's publication I have used it in writing workshops, online classes, and college classrooms. I have gone on to write more books on writing. Christi's oldest child recently married. I am a grandmother. As friends, Christi and I continue to write to each other (usually by email now) about our new ventures in life. Together and apart, we have witnessed excellent writing from people inspired by the exercises and discussions we wrote into *Convertible*. Over the years, we have heard from people across the country who use the book—professors at the Conference On College Composition and Communication, journalists, novelists, picture book writers, and the yet-to-be published who have attended conferences such as the Pacific Northwest Writer's Conference, held near where our book idea hatched. "When I read this, I feel like I can do it!" is the common response we get. It makes us smile.

It took publication of the first edition of the book for our story to find its twelfth chapter, included in this edition. And it took a couple years more for Chapters 13 and 14 to come about. Writing can't be hurried. Life events bring the news an author wants to digest. We are delighted to have the opportunity to once again share what we learned with those for whom writing is now at least a glimmer in their eyes and also with those for whom it is already one of their deepest passions.

Our message: Yes, you can do it.

Here is our experience figuring out how we did it and what helped most.

chapter one

The Bus:
How do we get started writing and keep going?

April 29

Dear Christi,

    Once I dreamt a boyfriend and I were on an English double decker bus. The bus driver spun around in his seat and faced us. He was blind-folded and continued to drive the bus. I was seized with panic.

    Waking, I remembered my boyfriend said something the day before about going forward on blind faith. The dream must certainly have expressed my fears about "blind faith."

    Eight years later, urged on by my soon-to-be husband, I took the Parachute Jump at the World Expo in Vancouver,

British Columbia. The experience was as close to weightlessness as one can get. In the seconds it took to land, my upper back tensed, becoming hard as stone. Without a feeling of being grounded, of having weight, I had tried to hold myself up by becoming a mountain.

It isn't easy to "go with the flow" or to "let the universe support one" or to "tune in to your right path." Beginning a piece of writing is always an act of "blind faith." There is nothing on the page. I begin on the blind faith that I can write something, that I can continue writing, that somehow I will find the right and satisfying place to stop. When I am inventing, I must become weightless, tumbling around in my own imagination and experiences.

As an inventor, I try not to keep my feet in someone else's writing, beautiful as it may be. I consider other people's writing like a stream I can sit beside in the sunlight, with birds flying and singing above me, small clouds across a blue sky. I remember I feel good sitting there and that sitting there helps me take in the sunlight, the birds, the white clouds, the blue sky.

When I begin to shape my inventions, I look at how other streams flow place to place. Then I insist that I face the blank page and begin my scribblings. I must share my early drafts and have trusted readers respond to my work, not critically but by noting first the parts that interest them because they stir emotions—empathy, sadness, joy, shock, regret, to name a few.

Next, I must hear from my trusted readers what places are unclear to them, what places raise distracting questions for the

Writing In A Convertible With The Top Down

readers or lead them away from their emotions. At this point, I must never listen to the words "good" and "bad." I am not looking for "constructive criticism" because in criticism of any kind there is separation and distinctions. I must receive response instead of criticism, because in response there is connection. Feeling connection with readers outside of ourselves is the most valuable tool we have for going on and shaping good writing.

Yours while the light is long,
Sheila

May 15

Dear Sheila,

Your letter makes me think about the books I've read lately—*Muggie Maggie*, by Beverly Cleary about a third grader who doesn't want to learn cursive writing; *The Island*, by Gary Paulsen about a teenager who escapes to an island to learn about the essence of loons, fish and himself; and *Family Pictures*, by Sue Miller, about the effect of an autistic child on a family.

What strikes me is that you can write about anything. Truly. Anything. But you don't have your story all at once. What you have usually is a kernel, an image that starts you off, that propels you.

I'm on the northbound 75 Metro bus. I'm looking at the driver, his bald head, his hairy arms and heavy, paw-like hands as he cranks the bicycle-tire-size steering wheel around and around. This has jarred my memory of my bus driver at Housman Elementary in Houston, Texas. I'd sit quietly in my window seat, a fifth grader who often daydreamed on the bus ride home, and watch Mr. Johnson peer into his mirror at roughhousers and tell us all to, "Shut up!"

That's a kernel.

I remember more about when I was a fifth grader...how my dad yelled at Mom every night as I lay in bed and I cried and scratched viciously at my mosquito bites. Then he'd come and check on us, and if I was awake, I'd have to kiss him good-night, tell him I loved him.

There's another image. Maybe I lived in a time and place where men didn't hold their anger back around the defenseless. Maybe by writing about these images, a story could grow about the effect of anger on childhood. This seems hard. It's a long journey.

Recently I dreamed I was bent over in a field, hunting for my computer. It had my latest book on it and it was lost in the soil somewhere. I plowed up the dirt all night looking; then I wrote this poem when I woke up:

> *Where is my computer?*
> *I fret the night long.*
> *It's been taken from*
> *My pack, my back, which is sore.*
> *my work-tired spine*

The labors of my mind
All gone and lost and can't be bought
At some computer store.

And then last night I dreamed there was this huge, disgusting, purplish pimple on my head. It was almost a boil. I squeezed it, pinching it fiercely, and out popped a story!

Time to transfer buses,
Christi

May 22

Dear Christi,

We may occupy our minds with fear and dread of losing our stories or not being able to find them, but they'll keep on growing if we return to the first kernel.

One idea I use for gathering images is to get "goof balls" flying. I start with any thought at all: Mom opened a can of worms this morning. The sky was violet when I went to bed and chartreuse when I woke up. I ask myself:

> Who might say something like that?
> Where would they be when they said it?
> What would they be doing?
> Who would their friends be?
> What would their home look like?
> Would they have a pet? What kind?

Tossing zany, or even painful, images around, like the ones you came up with on the bus, is like taking the cap off a full ketchup bottle and turning the bottle upside down.

It's messy, but it's the fastest way. Censoring ideas is like screwing the cap back on and putting the bottle in a deep freeze. Censor one idea and ten others back away from your tongue and your fingers.

Once you have the image, it's your connection to developing the story. The kernel directs the writing. If you stick with it, it becomes a map to a whole new territory of writing possibilities.

Ready for the drive,
Sheila

A KEY: DRIVE YOUR OWN ROUTE

Driving your own route means following the roads you find yourself on when you set out to write and trusting them to take you somewhere. But lots of times when we want to write, we don't even seem to be able to start the ignition. And then if we can start, we don't know how to keep our gas pedal down. And then if we can keep the pedal down, we may get into some sort of a word fog and not see the road we are driving on.

TAKE IT FOR A SPIN

Here are two writing practices to help you.

First, let's do some goofballs. They may seem like nonsense, but they are really "what ifs." What if the sky were chartreuse when I woke up and pink when I went to bed? What would I make of it? What would it mean to me? What if I threw a package away and saw a genie grow from my garbage can? What would I say? What might the genie say? What sex would the genie be? What plans would I make with the genie? Make a list of what ifs. Fill a whole page. Then choose one you would really like to explore. Make up a bunch of questions for yourself. When you feel ready, shift from the questions to writing some answers. Narrate the event and what results from it. Stop when you feel satisfied.

Another way to create some goofballs is to think "sometimes" as Sheila did for a poem she wrote:

SOMETIMES WHEN I KISS YOU

I see blue flowers,
and sometimes a young girl
in party dress, hair
fastened with roses.
You ask if she is
picking the flowers. The flowers

*are wild and I never see
what she does with her hands.*

When you are writing a "sometimes" you do not need to be intimidated about whether what you are writing is true or not. Sometimes it is true, even if that is just at the moment you are writing it down.

Write a long list of "sometimes"—sometimes when I walk through the supermarket all the fish start jumping, sometimes when my phone rings I think the President is calling me for advice, sometimes when the mailman hasn't arrived on time, I think there is a court injunction on my mail, sometimes when.... Fill the page.

Now look back at your favorite sometimes. You can extend that thinking.

If, for instance, you had written in your list, "Sometimes when the petunia blossoms shrivel in the heat from lack of water, I think I've been given the job of executioner," you might choose to continue on about the many times in your life that you feel responsible and lacking and think negatively about yourself. You might write more "sometimes" that are in the same vein as the one you chose—for instance, "Sometimes when the kids don't clean their room I think the behavior police are going to jail me for incompetency. Sometimes when a guest pours milk into their coffee and it curdles because it's gone sour, I think the health department will fine me." With this kind of writing you are using specific images and details and your writing will be interesting.

You are driving your own bus; you will find which roads to take as you go along.

As with all of the writing practices offered in this book, you may address your writing to us if you'd like. We found that addressing our writing to one another always gave us a place to start and the feeling that our writing really mattered:

> Dear Christi and Sheila,
> Sometimes when I...

After you do a letter to us, you may want to choose another sometimes and put it in the mouth of a character or in a narrator's voice. You can start a story in this way. Just let the narrator or the character say the sometimes and go where that takes you.

chapter two

Peonies:
How do we continue our enthusiasm for writing day after day?

May 30

Dear Sheila,

    I love springtime in Seattle.

    My husband, Bill, and I and the girls went out to a peony farm yesterday; ten-thirty on a cool Memorial Day weekend morning, raindrops still dripping from the thousands of huge red and pink and white peonies, a long-haired woman bent over weeding between the rows, smoke from the garden house stove floating up against the backdrop of pine and cedar trees, its smell mingling with the perfume of the flowers.

The pom-pom flowers of the peonies can be the size of Volleyballs! (Bill says I exaggerate, but they *seem* that big.) Doubles and triples, and such rich colors. Too bad they're in bloom only a month or so out of the entire year.

I laughed when I read a quote by Ann Lovejoy on the list of varieties the nursery handed out: "Flower time at A & D Peony Nursery is pretty special, and the sight of several acres of these buxom creatures blossoming their ruffled heads off is worth the trip—*"Buxom!"* That's the word for them.

Yours in exaggeration,
Christi

June 6

Dear Christi,

My kids and husband are off on trips, so the house is mine for the weekend. I've moved my computer onto the kitchen table. From the open window, a breeze blows over me, rustling the paper piled behind my printer.

From my window I see the cherry trees in my backyard. I think about the cycles to watch in a fruit tree—February blossoming, then flower hips growing rounded, deep green foliage in late spring, red cherries against those leaves in summer.

I think of my husband climbing the garage roof, the telephone pole, the ladder and the fence as he forages for food, my son raking cherry leaves in fall, me staring at the eloquence of bare branches in winter, my daughter collecting blossom petals from the lawn each spring.

It doesn't matter that the cherries last only a few weeks—all the rest is fruit, too.

By the buxom window,
Sheila

A KEY: WRITE THROUGH ALL THE SEASONS

Writing through all the seasons means not waiting only for the times something important comes our way and we are absolutely propelled to write (that may only happen a few weeks out of the year, like the peonies blooming). We can fall into the trap of thinking we can only write about something that is very precious and then it seems hard to find something valuable enough to write about. Other times we may find something weighty enough to write about (like love or the meaning of life) and realize we can't tackle such a big topic.

However, we can always write from our experience, inner and outer. Writing through all the seasons means continually noticing what is around us and noticing how what is around us sparks our memories.

TAKE IT FOR A SPIN

A good place to start writing is by a window. As an observer you will become aware of the processes around you. Don't be afraid to enjoy exaggeration as Christi does. Writers often put a magnifying glass to the particular event, object, or person they are noticing. They really look and enjoy it.

What do you see outside your window? An alley with trash? A lawn that needs cutting? Cars parked and cars zooming past?

Write about where you are and what you see. Write about how what is outside the window got to be there, how it will change, and how it will come back again—dandelions in the lawn send their bright flowers up, lose them to the lawn-mower, send their seeds on white parachutes again; cars zoom, park, pull out and zoom away. Ask yourself, "What can be measured by the cycle I have discussed?" My moods? Friendships? What?

Don't worry about whether you are making sense. Let the images capture you. Let them present themselves and be included. Then just write what thoughts are awakened in you in response to the questions we have asked. Your mind will be making connections on a deep level. Trust this and let yourself write.

This is a good exercise to do frequently, perhaps in a journal. Each time you write for this exercise, you may want to put the writing away and look at it only after time has gone by. You will notice you have built a storehouse of captured moments of deep reflection.

chapter three

Garbage:
How do we overcome
writer's block?

June 10

Dear Sheila,

    I'm stuck. I had a dream last week that I was trapped in a garbage depot with huge red garbage trucks and bins threatening me. Squalid water was behind me, the road I'd come down to the depot on was, alas, one-way (not that I wanted to return on it) and the only stairway out that I could see I didn't want to take. The owner was a sleazy salesman who, I knew, would charge me dearly to use his stairs. I couldn't tell what was beyond the large hill that blocked me in, either. I just knew I wanted to be on the other side.

Joseph Campbell, in his book *Hero with a Thousand Faces*, describes this moment as "a call to adventure." He talks about how we go along in life until "the familiar life horizon has been outgrown; the old concepts, ideals, and emotional patterns no longer fit; the time for passing of a threshold is at hand."

I do have glimmers that my stuckness is part of a journey, and that it won't work to scramble around frantically, beating my head on the trucks. What will work?

It occurs to me that being still and experiencing the stuckness is all I can do. Perhaps I can write about it as a way of experiencing it. What is its color? Shape? Size? Where does it live? Who is keeping it there or why does it stay? How does it approach me? What do I do when it comes near?

I can also ask myself if it is time to be doing something differently. What would I like to be writing? How would I like to be writing it? Is there some aspect of my life I want to change? How could I live differently? I can write about this! As Campbell says, "What is your bliss?" I would add the word *now*. What is your bliss now?

Lifting the big, black hood,
Christi

June 15
Dear Christi,
I drove up to my house after dropping off my husband's suit at the cleaners (shaving cream on it from decorating a bridal

car over the weekend) and picking up groceries for my son's classmates, who will be turning our living room into a home video studio this afternoon to tape a talk show on heavy matters (the Israeli-Arab conflict).

Just as I wished, the mail basket was nicely stuffed. The grocery bag sat on the porch while I sorted through the envelopes. After reading the news that my friend once again received a $1000 Individual Artist Grant from the Arts Commission and I felt that jealousy I sometimes do, I saved your envelope for inside and lugged the bag full of pop and cookies to the kitchen.

Today was garbage day and I remembered to get the kitchen garbage out before collection time. Weekly, I sort through the bottles, cans and paper, I keep in my kitchen, take them to the curb in the Easter green and yellow plastic baskets the city has given us for recycling. I feel somehow pleased by this passage of materials through my house. I see our household as a plant performing entry-level processing.

Last week I got so inspired, I brought household toxic waste (paint thinner, flea spray and batteries) to a once-a-year community clean up I had never gone to before. There were cars for blocks and blocks waiting to drive in with trunk loads of stuff.

But already we stockpile for another year. More used batteries are in the drawer, and life goes on. The bride and groom return from their honeymoon this weekend. I'll get the suit from the cleaners in a few days. Over the weeks, my son's teenage friends will drink many six packs of Coke as they discuss the world's problems for their assignments. I will spend more time on the garbage (Do you know farm families are able to use a whole pig and throw away nothing, not even whiskers which they use for broom bristles?)

But always, as you remind me, in the midst of what we think of as our lives is our inner life to which we must pay attention if we are to know ourselves and really feel that we live.

Your dream of red trucks and bins is so vivid, the sleazy salesman placed by the stairs. Is he the person inside each one of us to whom we are always in danger of selling out by going in a direction just because others want us to, or worse, because we're afraid of our bosses? He extorts such a huge price to use the stairs because it is so costly to our souls when we move without our inner lives' consent.

"Nothing is wasted" a wise friend of mine says. Perhaps in the "call to adventure" you mention, our own first task is as garbage collectors who must find a way to recycle what's threatening us, use what seems to be waste. Staying stuck at the garbage depot forces us to look into the bins. I'll bet you my recycling baskets that if we can do this, the large hill will open before us.

Just writing to you in reflection about your dream, I feel my jealousy toward my grant winning friend easing somewhat. I feel the affirmation again that the process of writing is what matters most for me, the joy I get when images gather, when "rewinding" through my day and life, I do not stop until every image that is important to the process has helped me work my way toward some small resolution, toward new understanding.

I close now remembering the smiling, impish face of my friend's two-year-old a couple of weeks ago as she chuckled and chanted like a fat Buddha, "Garbageman, garbageman, garbageman."

Riding the red trucks,
Sheila

A KEY: RECYCLE THE INNER LIFE

So often when we're stuck, we think of fleeing. But as ancient wisdom advises, the way out is the way in. This is what we mean when we say to recycle the inner life. Just as plants recycle the carbon dioxide released when organic life decays by changing it into food, so we recycle our inner life into energy for moving forward. This is done in details.

TAKE IT FOR A SPIN

Look at any stuckness in your life as you would look at food on your plate, your face when getting ready for an important date, a person you haven't seen in a long time. Take in the details through your senses. How do things look, feel, taste, sound and smell?

Think of anywhere that you have been stuck—in traffic, with a date you don't like, in your house because you're sick, with too much work to do. As long as you're stuck there, take this time to really look at where you are.

Write about that date's nose.

Write about the laundry pile that you won't get to.

Write about the drivers in the cars surrounding you.

The writing will tell you how rich your experience is. The jam will clear, the date will turn amusing, the stay at home will become okay.

chapter four

Molasses:
Where does the meaning in a story come from?

June 20

Dear Sheila,

"An expert is somebody who is more than 50 miles from home, has no responsibility for implementing the advice he gives, and shows slides." (Edwin Meese, *New York Times*, January 24, 1984).

Now that I've been asked to speak about writing once again, this time at a teachers' conference in Yakima this fall, I'm apprehensive as always. What am I going to say? According to Ed Meese, I qualify as an expert, but to tell you the truth, thinking about myself in the role of "guru" clogs me up for some reason.

It seems that after I understand something new and share it, I get locked in. I get narrower. Somehow, in the "holy" act of sharing, I lose the mystery and excitement of discovery and become the mouthpiece, the expert.

In the Chinese *Tao-te Ching:* "He who thinks he knows, doesn't know. He who knows that he doesn't know, knows. For in this context, to know is not to know. And not to know is to know."

Bogged down in expert city,
Christi

June 24

Dear Christi,

I have a game that teaches us to be large. I borrowed it from *Teaching Poetry to Children*, an exercise book written by David Greenberg.

It is a game using metaphor. To draw a metaphor is to admit that the essence of something may not ever be wholly described, but it can be experienced and felt in comparison to something else we know and feel. There is self-enlarging power in recognizing that what makes one thing like another thing is that *you* experience it that way—earrings are like tetherballs; a grapefruit is like a planet; a purse, one student of mine said, is like a coffin. Our world takes on texture, size, and shape when we allow ourselves to draw such likenesses in our experience.

How freeing it is not to add any reasons—that is, not to explain an earring is like a tetherball because sometimes a little round gold ball swings on a little gold string. Give me my metaphors straight—yes, when you put in like, technically you are using simile. It ruins my experiencing of the world, though, to label what I'm doing. Distinguishing between metaphor and simile when your heart wants to experience and write is like stopping to remember which food groups are represented in the piece of cherry pie you are about to eat.

My poet friend James Mitsui reminds us that often we were censored for metaphorical language. We may have said as a child, "Look at the fingernail moon" and been told the moon is not a fingernail. We may have decided to never again "confuse" a small fingernail we know up close with the mysterious and distant moon.

Now even scientists admit that what they find are ultimately only metaphors for what can't be seen. Metaphor is powerful thinking for interpreting the world, and it is a lovely, freeing way of seeking truth.

I challenge myself to ten "likes" a day. I notice something and put "is like" after it: a window is like, a parking space is like, a nasturtium is like, the crows on the telephone wire are like. Later a good comparison pops into my head. A window is like an ice skating pond, a parking space is like the space between my own front teeth, a nasturtium is like a basketball, crows on a telephone wire are like clothespins.

Knowing a letter is like a menu,
Sheila

June 28

Dear Sheila,

My stuckness is filling me with lethargy, like molasses poured into my veins. Lassitude, sluggishness, who-gives-a-rip stuporville.

When I finish a book, I start looking around at what else is out there, novels, philosophy books, religion. Eventually my stories seem silly to me, inconsequential. They aren't myths! They're not going to save the world! I start taking notes from my reading, writing down quotations and analyzing how someone puts a theme into a story, as if this will make my next book more consequential. It's overwhelming. I want to write a good story with all of that deep stuff operating in the background where I can't see it. I can't hold it all in my head.

I'm reminded of a poem that I wrote in third grade:

> *Snowflakes falling through the air*
> *Like little pairs of underwear.*
> *Down, down, down,*
> *To the little village town*
> *Where my mother said,*
> *"If you want to go skating on the river,*
> *You'd better eat your liver."*

Wanting to skate again on the river,
Christi

Writing In A Convertible With The Top Down

July 1

Dear Christi,

Letters from you keep arriving like cars down the freeway.

No wonder you remember your poem. Worrying that your stories are inconsequential and trying to *force* the deep stuff into them is like a little girl gagging down her liver before she can go skating.

The deep stuff is something you have to count on as a writer. If it weren't there, our poems and stories wouldn't sound right, but it's not that we can set out to write about the deep stuff. When we're writing well, the deep stuff informs our choices and guides the work. Once I wrote "our dreams choose us." The deep stuff chooses the story.

I like your poem. I like the wonderful leap of association from snowflakes to pairs of underwear, a leap that only the unconscious, keeper of all the "deep stuff," makes easily. In the underwear I feel how vulnerable a child is, how all encompassing that vulnerability is because it falls all over town. But no sooner do I feel the largeness of the vulnerability, then the conscious mind barges in announcing the necessity of eating liver.

Don't be hard on yourself—think about those little pairs of underwear, the Christi who thought them up looking at the snow. Stay with them. That's where the deep stuff is.

Thinking of you as I
go to fold the laundry,
Sheila

A KEY: SWEETEN IT WITH METAPHOR

As writers, we may feel our work is plodding and lifeless. Sweeten it with metaphor means bringing our subjects alive by refreshing our experience of them. We like it when a writer lets us experience his or her perception by comparing it to something we know but may never before have associated with the subject. We like apt descriptions. Metaphor is a way to precisely evoke experience without interfering with that experience. Sweetening it with metaphor means creating a treat for ourselves and for others. When you do this, your writing will have the sweetening properties of molasses, not the properties of how it moves.

TAKE IT FOR A SPIN

Contemporary American poet Robert Hass shares a writing exercise in his poetry workshops that helps writers cultivate their use of metaphorical thinking. His writing exercise is taken from the rhythmic work-dialogue of the Abantu people of Africa. There a man might say, "The sound of a tusk cracking." The person working beside him might answer, "The anger of a hungry man," Robert Hass quoted from *Technicians of the Sacred: A Range of Poetry from Africa, America, Asia, Europe and Oceania* by Jerome Rothenberg.

The principle used by the Abantu is one of internal comparison, a dialogue the imagination has with itself, one statement sparking another, not by logic, but by intuition.

Students of Sheila's have written:

The sun set behind the mountains
A child ducking behind the sofa

A broken chair
The disappointed parent

Challenge yourself to write these couplets, alone or in a group. Write down a list of first lines from what you or your group see—boys playing soccer on the field, ducks preening by the lake, blackberry jam on toast... Now fill in second lines as they come to you.

Don't censor yourself. Write many second lines to the same first line. Which ones are exciting? You will know the ones that offer a refreshed perception of the world by a little rush of feeling. When this kind of couplet is working well, the listener feels a body sensation, an "ah," or a deep smile, or an "oh!"

Be sure your second lines come from a completely different landscape than your first line. Never try to involve cause and effect. Remember we are being intuitive, working with metaphors. For instance, "a dime on the table top" answered by "a circle on a rectangle" is not very refreshing. It is more a function of the categorizing brain taking over and classifying the images. "A dime on the table top" answered by "I will get some chewing gum" is cause and effect. It does not effectively refresh my vision of the world. "A dime on the table top/first star in the night sky" is offers the comparison you are looking for in this exercise. The desk and the night sky are not from the same landscape and so our vision of both is refreshed.

Now it's your turn.

chapter five

Beach House:
How do writers get the
conscious mind to m<u>el</u>d
with the <u>unconscious?</u> *huh?*

July 3

Dear Sheila,

Here I am at the beach. I just set Annie Rose and Molly up outside with their paints and rocks—rock painting at the beach is a major pastime.

I'm thinking about inside and outside. Inside the cabin, outside on the beach; inside the car traveling to get here, Bill outside walking each morning for exercise. My feelings inside, the reality of the situation outside (which I'll probably never truly understand). The painted creations outside on the picnic bench, the intention of what they are meant to look like inside the minds of Annie Rose and Molly.

Every story has this inside and outside part, at least any story that has richness and can sustain a reader's interest. So when I start with the story idea, whatever piece it might be, I can't go very far without uncovering the other side. It takes two ideas to write a story, rubbing against each other, creating sparks and fire.

Sometimes I start with the outside idea, as I did with *Rusty Fertlanger, Lady's Man*. I saw an article in the newspaper about a ninth-grade boy who had to wrestle a girl. A lot of the outside story (plot) was right there in the article—coach gives boy a choice, but if boy decides not to wrestle, he forfeits. Boy decides to wrestle, girl pins him, his friends give him a bad time. Okay. But that is a newspaper article. Reporting. It is a plot. This happens then that happens and so on.

The thing that turns this into fiction, into a *story*, is the other idea (as well as the character, of course). I ended up pairing this plot with the idea that Rusty was a cartoonist especially interested in superhero comic books—and the idea that the masculinity portrayed in these books (and therefore what Rusty believes is true manliness) is a lie—to create the inner storyline, the inside idea.

Inside, looking out,
Christi

July 6

Dear Christi,

I think of you and your children painting rocks on the beach. What a wise mom those girls have who encourages them in their messy endeavors! We must have a place developed in ourselves that respects and enjoys art's messiness or we will never grow the stories and poems, dances and songs, paintings and sculptures whose seeds are planted in all of us.

I don't think there is a person born who doesn't have the capacity of "design mind"—the pattern seeking, mystical, dream mind that knows something of the true nature of existence. Early in life we are taught to ignore that mind, to think of our dreams and stories as at best hobbies, to "learn a vocation that pays well," to obey rather than create, to "work" rather than "fritter our time away" on creative pursuits.

The measure of just how very thoroughly we as a culture play down our design mind is how rich and how famous we make actors, singers, novelists and personalities who catch on. How much more parity if everyone's creativity were cultivated. Art would not be a spectator sport.

We can nurture the confidence to listen for our design mind. Your way of expressing the structure of fiction writing is superlative—the inside and outside story. I like thinking of that. If we encourage ourselves, we will find the "magical weld" because that's how our design mind works. We are all graced with the gift of it. Some of us have not buried it. All of us must be encouraged to reclaim it.

Going to water the seeds
outside and within,
Sheila

JULY 8

Dear Sheila,

Here's a funny metaphor for you. The beach cabin we're staying in here at Hood Canal is paneled with pine tongue-in-groove. The kind with the spattering of large and small brown knots from ceiling to floor. My mother and her younger sister shared a room with such paneling in their youth. One night Mom was gazing at the walls and she said to Emme, "You see those brown spots? Do you know what they are?" Emme did not know. She was ten years younger than Mom. "They're farts," my mother explained. "Every time you fart, it goes right up there on the wall. Little ones make little farts, big ones...." Mom looked at Emme's stunned, but believing face, and added, "If you don't stop, the whole wall will be covered with 'em." Emme went crying to Grandma, who thirty years later related the story to me. A good metaphor is a source of repeated delight.

Still smiling,
Christi

Writing In A Convertible With The Top Down

July 10

Dear Christi,

Yes, a funny story. However, I identify with the younger sister who went running to her mother, humiliated and frightened by all the farts past, present and future, on the wall!

My empathy for the younger sister reminds me of what I have had to overcome in order to write. One way or another my mother was always telling me how "dirty" I'd make the world unless I was "nice." In its root, the word nice means "not to know."

We can't write meaningfully if we are trying to be nice. I remember writing empty letters to pen pals about how nice everything in my life was. I got a new dress! My social studies teacher gave me an A! I remember the profound flatness I felt writing this despite the exclamation points. My heart was actually breaking with sadness from my parents' constant arguing, from my feeling unsure about their marriage and myself in a new school. I couldn't write well because I couldn't write things as they were because they were like farts on the wall that weren't nice.

Art doesn't exclude the unpleasant. It faces it. I'd like to follow these characters, the sisters ten years apart, on their journeys through life.

Yours as I imagine picking
up a novel about them,
Sheila

JULY 11

Dear Sheila,

I'm still at the beach, as you can tell by my watercolor-painted envelope. I've been seized by creativity. Painting envelopes, *making* envelopes, inventing a new pasta dish with olive oil and tomatoes. I know it's all byproduct of this story that's building. The energy is there, pulsing inside me, seeing ways to improvise for lack of butter and 2% milk and a screwy washing machine. You use olive oil and jam, mix nonfat with cream and type letters next to the washing machine so that you can nudge the knob from wash to rinse to spin dry! You adapt. I adapt. And it's fun.

There were two families in the cabin next door over the weekend: two sets of parents with two children each. One of the fathers caught my attention. He had boundless energy. He rallied the kids, including my two, into game after game, activity after activity. His voice was very distinctive, sort of nasal-ish but not abrasive. I knew where he was at any given moment of the weekend, and if I didn't hear him, he was inside or out fishing. He was like an otter. A daddy otter. He even had a mustache.

I found myself wondering what this man did for a living, where he was raised, how he met his wife (who was very cute, but not nearly so friendly as her husband) what he liked to read, etc. Do you ever do this? I become intensely nosy about someone. I want to know all of his or her business. Does he pay off all his bills immediately, or is he in VISA debt? Does he cut his toenails off straight across as my husband does, or does he cut them to conform to the shape of the cuticle?

When I create a character, I almost always begin with the shadow of someone I know, or imagine that I know. I know enough about this father to use him as a minor character someday. Main characters are a different thing altogether. I have to know or make up answers to all of my questions.

I begin, as Muriel Spark says in *Loitering With Intent*, by "fixing a fictional presence in my mind's eye, then adding a history to it." That's the work I think I'm doing right now. I think my fictional presence is a 12-year-old boy who loves animals. Just saying this is like shooting electric current through me. I'm nervous, I'm interested, I'm jittery. I want to be writing this kid's story. But I know I've got to play some games to pull him out of my unconscious.

I've used all kinds of stuff, tricks, in the past. Astrology books (I look up the sign I guessed the character to be and read the description), magazine pictures and pictures of old classmates in yearbooks (who look like my character might look), name books. I find myself reading similar books to what I imagine writing, trying to get a feel for my story. This is not plagiarism. This is priming the pump.

Sometimes I just start writing. Nonsense stuff, really. Just make up a name for this presence and write throwaway pages, to get me thinking, accepting and rejecting stuff. Improvising. Adapting. This is the trick that grabs me right now.

Off to write some
throwaway pages,
Christi

JULY 13

Dear Christi,

Your sentence about olive oil and jam, cream and nonfat milk, and writing by the washing machine got me thinking of a man I was with for awhile. He told me that he fell in love with me watching me bake a cake.

I had felt the urge to bake and I'd chosen my favorite quick cake recipe, then proceeded to discover I had few of the ingredients it required. But on the wings of the energy of desiring to create the cake, I found satisfactory substitutes for the missing ingredients. My favorite applesauce cake turned out, forty minutes later, to be cranberry bread.

Once recently the same man told me the story again and I remembered the rush of energy, how I solved my problems like a happy raft on the river's current.

Could it be like that always if I didn't fret? If I trusted that the river would come and carry me toward solution? If I remembered that I am "river worthy" and can work wonders when that current flows beneath me?

Taking cranberries
from the freezer,
Sheila

A KEY: COOK WITH WHAT YOU HAVE ON HAND

Cooking with what we have on hand means using the names, phrases, customs, and knowledge unique to our families and experience.

Christi's grandmother loved to cook oxtail soup. She called it offal soup. Offal is unpopular pieces of meat—the liver, intestine, tail, feet. Her husband used to bring these home from the slaughter house. When Christi was writing her book *All of the Above*, she assigned this knowledge to a fifth grader who made a complete meal for under a dollar using offal and got her Girl Scout cooking badge.

Sheila remembers her father's *tallit*, kept in a velvet case in his dresser drawer. In the Jewish religion, a *tallit*, or prayer shawl, may be given to a boy on his bar mitzvah. In a screenplay Sheila experimented with Neal becomes afraid of his prayer shawl because of the memory of his dead older brother's body wrapped in one. He even refuses to wear a jacket or to sleep under covers.

While Christi's husband was growing up, he shared a basketball pump needle with his brother. One of them was always misplacing it. Even though a new one was only ten cents, buying it was out of the question. Now, whenever he realizes he is denying himself something small—an extra stapler, magic marker, can opener, or scissors—he cries, "I'm doing another basketball needle!"

Don't forget how loaded you are with these memories. Use them in your writing whether you write a personal experience piece or assign characters your memory tidbits. Either way, writing these tidbits can lead to surprising unconscious themes. Offal is the unwanted, the leftover. In the book, the girl turned that into success and gained satisfaction. The *tallit* is a prayer shawl and a shroud. In the screenplay, the boy comes to understand that to have a beginning acknowledges that there will be an ending. The basketball needle is a symbol of scrimping, denying oneself easier passage in the world. Maybe someday Christi will use it in a story.

TAKE IT FOR A SPIN

Take some time now to let yourself explore the cupboards of your memory. What are the sayings, objects, rituals, foods and events that are on hand for you? List them, fill as much of a page as you can.

Now choose one to explore with all the remembered details of time and place. Write a page or two describing the memory.

Ask yourself why you chose the particular subject you wrote about. Ask yourself how it relates to what you are experiencing in your life right now. Why did you remember it? Why did it attract you? How can you use it to evoke the essence of your current experience?

Sometimes we tap the unconscious as we begin a piece of writing, but other times we need to call in our unconscious when we are in the middle of a piece. We may not immediately know how characters would behave or how to show the consistency in their personalities, or we may not know what actions would surely cause certain behaviors. How can we go on writing when we don't know the answers?

The unconscious can help here, but, like an oyster, it needs an irritating grain of sand before it can create a jewel.

The grain is a specific question. What are you after? What do you need here? You are trying to figure out what it is you're writing about! You must back away for a second and brainstorm questions about your characters. It's scary because you don't know the answers, but you have to pose the question—How does Irene's blackmail really work? What is at stake for the blackmailer and the blackmailee? Why does it feel desperate to them?

Once you've posed the questions (you might deal only with one or two of these at a time), leave the place where you are writing. Go shopping, wash the dishes, take a walk, sleep, whatever, to give your unconscious a chance to form the pearl. Something you hear on the radio or something said by passersby might answer the question. The unconscious is always working on it.

chapter six

Cherry Trees:
How do we use other people's writing to help ourselves write?

JULY 15

Dear Christi,

    Last night my husband began reading the letters of our correspondence. He was tired. When I walked into the room, he demanded, "I want information. I want to read this and find out how to write, see a shape." I didn't feel pleased to hear this. But I didn't feel any river of current beneath me carrying me toward a new solution.

    This morning I told my husband I was sorry he hadn't finished the letters. He took a shower, lay down and began to read again. I came into the room just as he set the letters down. This time he said, "They're so good that I'm inspired to write."

An hour later he placed this text in my hands:

> I am a large man yet I can disappear easily inside the cherry trees in our backyard. The leaves of these trees are thick and heavy and only occasionally betray my presence by a gentle rustling as I move from branch to branch. It's difficult for a man my size to hide, to escape the sight of others in the world. But in my cherry trees, I disappear into the arms of Eden and am provided for. I have been in the trees, happy and eating the delicious fruit while my wife was in the backyard asking the kids if they had seen me or knew where I was off to. It is a dark pleasure to escape the bonds of care. I imagine Rapture to be this kind of pleasure—to leave the others behind in their world of concerns for the land of heaven.
>
> The cherries appear every year around the 4th of July. They are the dark sweet kind, the kind that are used for exquisite chocolate covered cherries, not the frivolous maraschino cherries that decorate sundaes. I love to climb these trees and lie in their branches and eat the

Writing In A Convertible With The Top Down

sweet flesh of that fruit. The larger tree ripens about two weeks before the smaller one, giving a "cherry season" of about three weeks. But in these arms, I imagine that it lasts all year long. I am Adam before the fall, living in the beauty of the earth and eating God's gifts without thought of toil and trouble. I reflect on how easy life can be. My wife and I hardly think of these trees the rest of the year. We don't spray them or fertilize or water them, yet they provide this crimson bounty for us year after year. I want life to be easy, and for three weeks a year, I can convince myself that it is.

I have no idea where the "bowl of cherries" metaphor comes from. I don't want a bowl of cherries. I want trees of cherries. Cherries in a bowl will only last a day or two—trees of cherries last for years. My wife and I have disagreements about how the cherries should be eaten. She likes to make pies and cobbler and I only want to gobble them as I pick them. Since she is so short, she depends on me to pick them for her desserts. There's nothing wrong with cherry cobbler, except that you have to pick the cherries, take the pits out, get all the pots and pans out, mix the batter and bake them. You usually make more than one mealtime's dessert in a recipe, so until it's eaten, you have this large baking pan of syrupy cherries and cherry soaked crumbs decorating your kitchen counter. How much better to pick the cherries, pop them in your mouth, spit the pits onto the ground and eat until you are satisfied. Then when you are hungry again, you climb the tree and there are more cherries still fresh and beautiful, hanging from the branches.

This is making something new from the same old ingredients. *Voilá*. Somehow the river starts flowing beneath the next person, too!

Paddling downstream,
Sheila

July 20

Dear Christi,

My daughter Emily saw Kurt's piece of writing lying on the butcher block in the kitchen. She read it and asked to read our letters. So we went out to the Honey Bear Café, drank steamed milk and *au laits*. She began reading our correspondence exclaiming, "Oh, my friend Airi would like this. My English teacher, Mr. Williams, would like to read this. He'd fill up a big mug with coffee early in September and sit in an armchair and read the whole thing in one sitting." Well, what could be better than such an enthusiastic critic? She went home and wrote and here it is:

> The Chinook salmon stacked head to tail are impressive merchandise as are the crabs with their many legs tied together. My mother and great grandmother are deciding whether to buy some while the clerk makes a show of throwing the fish to the man at the cash register. Each fish lands with a satisfying sound like an arrow hitting the target at camp this spring where I was the "archery lady" showing parents how to show their children how.
>
> The sound is solid without the doubt of the soft sound when I brush someone in a crowd and wonder if I should apologize. It also has dimension instead of the linear crack of the videotaped automobile accidents I watched in driver's ed.
>
> The salmon look like shoulders, strong without being hard. It is the solidity of living things, the way I feel when I run past the point where I think I can't go any further, the tenacity that keeps dandelion seeds from falling off before they're ready. I pick only the oldest for my

baby brother when he wants to release the flock of "sea gulls."

"We pack for up to 48 hours." My mom talks about sending one to my great grandmother when she's returned to Miami. The salmon's strength will be her food. Through her shoulders I can see the hardness of bone when she tells me that once she could go faster

Emily says, "The Chinook salmon stacked head to tail are impressive merchandise" was a line that popped into her head at the public market as we toured through the stalls. She ran through some possible paragraphs in her head and thought, "No, I don't want to write about that. Ill save the sentence for a letter to someone at camp."

But when she got home after finishing our correspondence, she let herself go with the line not knowing where it would lead her. She laid down her new writing with a smile, "For lots of people what isn't is a not, but for you guys, what isn't is only a not yet."

Our cherries are gone from the tree now, but their sweetness lingers on. The green leaves are thick and the branches growing.

Yours in the summertime,
Sheila

A KEY: EAT THE DELICIOUS FRUIT OF OTHER WRITING

Writers often read in a state of hunger for something delicious. They want to admire, eat and digest the elegant strategies of other people's writing.

Christi has a giant appetite for novels since that is her genre. She notices how books often present a metaphor to sum up a character's situation:

In Betsy Byars' *The Pinballs*, three foster children have bounced from home to home.

In Elizabeth Jolley's *The Newspaper of Claremont Street*, the residents of the street lean on the cleaning woman they all employ for news about each other.

In Paula Danziger's *The Divorce Express*, life for ninth grader Phoebe is like the bus ride she takes back and forth between her parents' homes.

TAKE IT FOR A SPIN

You have just read writing by Sheila's husband and her daughter that also uses metaphor. They have addressed concerns and philosophies in their lives by describing something they experience through their senses. Eat the delicious fruit and be energized in your own writing. Here's a writing exercise based on Christi's observation to speed you on your way:

Think of something you do or see—shooting baskets, changing a diaper, setting the table, the telephone, a basket of fruit. Write a paragraph, going into detail about what you hear, smell, taste, touch, and observe while doing or seeing what you have chosen to discuss.

Now ask, "How does what I'm writing seem to me to also describe a current concern or desire in life?" If you have described playing basketball, for instance, you may find that what you've said suggests a philosophy about solving a major problem in your life or evokes the feelings of asking a particular person to do something for you, or seems like when you prepare to ask something of your boss. Write about this.

Don't think too hard when you begin. Then to recap: select something you feel connected to, describe it using your experience of it through the five senses. Let what you have written suggest a major concern or life desire; explore it using the writing you did as a metaphor.

Here's another writing exercise to try: read a poem or piece of excerpt from a piece of prose you like, then put the book down and immediately write whatever comes to mind. In your writing, use the images and memories that are with you just after you leave off reading. These will come naturally as you associate images you just read with images from your own experience and present surroundings.

chapter seven

The Bridge on the River Kwai: How does a writer visualize the structure of a story?

August 7

Dear Sheila,

I'm mourning the beach. Something about the way time passed there, about the flow of the day. Saying a day passed slowly or sped by is foreign to me when I'm there. The tides, meals, and the normal changes in my body as the day progresses (aching back and caffeine headaches included) seem a more elemental way to mark the day, as opposed to the newspaper, the TV, the phone and the mail. At the beach, the day's shape is comfortable.

Interesting that Kurt would criticize the letters, cry out for information, then produce such a nice piece. Have you ever noticed how people sometimes act angry when they're inspired? Like they have to lash out? I'm certainly that way sometimes. Let me work! Leave me alone! I don't know what in the hell I'm doing! I need information!!

Kurt is right. The angry Kurt. Writing does need a shape, a beginning, middle, end. Highs and lows of action. Climaxes, rug-pulls, black moments, dénouements.

Making every scene move the action along as well as reveal character. That all sounds so impossible!

There is a tool I use when I'm writing a book. It's my kind of outline. I learned it from one of my friends who brainstorms her books with a clustering, circle method. She does a cluster for each of her characters, showing relationships, like this:

Each relationship—how these people feel about one another and why—is a subplot. She also makes one for plot, like this:

```
┌──────────────┐        ┌──────────┐        ┌──────────────┐
│    Why?      │        │ Problem— │        │    How?      │
│What happened │ ◄────► │ Present  │ ◄────► │To solve problem│
│ to get in this│       │  crisis  │        │ what to do   │
│  situation   │        │          │        │              │
└──────────────┘        └──────────┘        └──────────────┘
```

I like to use the "W" outline that Pat Kubis and Bob Howland describe in *Writing Fiction, Nonfiction and How to Publish*. Basically it looks like this:

```
A_____D_____G
 \                      /  \                      /
  \                    /    \                    /
   \                  C      E                  /
    \                /        \                /
     \              /          \              /
      \           /              \           /
       \        /                  \        /
        B                            F
```

AG: Intent—protagonist wants something.

AB: First barrier—what stands in protagonist's way.

BC: First barrier reversal—protagonist does something to overcome first barrier.

CD: High point—looks like protagonist will get her intent.

DE: Rug pull—something happens to frustrate intent.

EF: Black moment—looks like all is lost—catastrophe.

FG: Resolution—protagonist goes on to achieve intent, through bravery, wit, etc.

My book *Rusty Fertlanger* fits this well, so I like to use it when I talk about writing. Not every piece of writing is so clear cut. But it's helpful to my shaping, forming, categorizing conscious mind to have some names to call parts of stories.

My husband, Bill, has heard writing terms umpteen times over the years of our marriage. At the risk of sounding like writing nerds, guess what Bill said a few weeks ago when we were watching his favorite movie—my first time seeing it—*Bridge on the River Kwai*? It was near the end, when the bomb has been set under the bridge and William Holden and his buddies are lying on the banks, sleeping. The tension of the night is gone, the dangerous work is done. All seems to be well, but then, horror of horrors, the river has gone down overnight and the bombs on the bridge as well as the line coming from the river to the detonator are exposed! Bill cringed visibly in his chair. "Isn't that the greatest rug pull in the movies?" he asked. It is good, I have to admit, but it's only the rug pull. The catastrophe or crisis is when Alec Guiness sees the bomb and decides to dismantle it and save the bridge.

There are lots of books about structuring fiction. One is *Structuring Your Novel: From Basic Idea to Finished Manuscript* by Robert C. Meredith and John D. Fitzgerald. You won't find anything more detailed than that book. It's useful to me sometimes, when my own personal tide is in and I have lots of pieces to plug into their various slots; other times, when my tide is out, I'm still playing with shadows.

Remembering the beach,
Christi

August 10

Dear Christi,

I tend to like the out-tide time myself. So much to look at, so much revealed for a short while, so much that will be covered by the tide again once it comes in. And when next the water goes out, everything may be rearranged! We do, I think, jump too quickly to "product" in our culture. It really is okay not to. It is enriching to anyone to stay with the "beach time"—that is what feeds us.

Sometimes, though, we want to store the nourishment, put it in a capsule that will allow us to put it on the shelves for others to take down and eat at a future date. We become like packagers and to do this, we must move from beach time into the kind of time you call newspaper, TV, phone and mail time. Demands of another order! Chronology, events, suspense, growth, setbacks, climax, resolution.

I have a reference to add to your bunch. Syd Field in *Screenplay* offers a paradigm for action: set up, plot point, confrontation, plot point, resolution. It looks like this:

```
              PLOT PT. 1      MID PT.      PLOT PT. 2
    |-----------|---------------|---------------|
    |  SET UP   |  CONFRONTATION |  RESOLUTION  |
    |-----------|---------------|---------------|
```

Set Up: The first part of a story or screenplay sets up the story. It introduces the characters and their situations. For instance, a little girl wants more than anything to go to a birthday party to which she was not invited. Her mother will be horrified if she crashes the party. The kids have not invited her because they think that being poor, she is stupid and unclean.

Plot point one: This must spin the action in a new direction—perhaps a puppy starts following the little girl and she hatches the idea that the puppy will make her more acceptable to the party crowd.

Confrontation: The little girl wants to get to the party and she uses the puppy in all kinds of ways to help her gain entrance but each time something gets in their way—perhaps she washes and dresses up the puppy only to get in terrific trouble with her mother for soiling the bathtub and she must clean the tub straight away. She then tries to teach the puppy to carry a bouquet of flowers in its mouth and she gets caught for picking the neighbors flowers and must sweep the neighbors walk in retribution further delaying her going to the party. You get it.

Midpoint: Midway in the confrontation something happens that will alter the course of the rest of the confrontations. Maybe in this case a shopkeeper entices the puppy with a bone. Now she must meet confrontations in getting "her" puppy back.

Plot point two: This spins the story again in a new direction. Maybe just as she's about to get the dog back, one of the rich popular kids comes strolling down the street toward the party and the puppy starts following him. Maybe he successfully brings the puppy to the party as a present for the hostess.

Resolution: The puppy entertains everyone at the party while the little girl watches from a window. Just as the little girl's mother is running down the street toward her daughter bent on spanking her for being so troublesome, a party guest shows up with a bouquet of flowers and the puppy grabs them from the vase they were put into and sniffs out the little girl and brings her the flowers. The mother is amazed at the magic of this event and the party goers are, too.

The little girl is invited in and her mother can't say no to an invitation.

Plot and subplot: Hmm. Okay, how to make the party itself more tied into the story of the little girl? You see the plot is simply a little girl wants to go to a party she was not invited to and gets in trouble trying, but is then accepted. Subplot usually has more theme and convolutions. Let's see, what do we have to work with here?

All the characters at the party, what their feuds are, what their tensions are—we can have a whole story here that also gets resolved by the action of the dog bestowing flowers on the little girl. What comes to mind is that they may have a storyteller at the party and he or she is telling a story about a dog who can always identify disguised princesses. The action of the puppy looks like an enactment of the story and all the kids are persuaded to think the little girl is actually a princess. The storyteller is the shopkeeper.

That is an off the top of my head example, but I believe we can do some good storytelling surprisingly easily.

Last night there was a total eclipse of the moon but there were too many clouds in the sky for us to see the "disc" moving off the moon, the shadow of our own planet. Maybe there is a writing lesson in the eclipse—is the best way to see ourselves by the shadows we create? And to see our shadows do we create three bodies—one illumines behind a second whose shadow falls on a third?

> Hoping a puppy will
> lay flowers at my feet,
> Sheila

A KEY: BUILD A SOLID STRUCTURE

You can learn a lot about structure by reading lots of stories and observing the following:

> What the author chooses to open the book with.
> Who tells the story (there may be more than one teller.)
> Whether you are watching the teller or thinking from inside the teller's head.
> Whether the teller knows what has happened, or finds it out as you read.
> Whether there are flashbacks and what triggers them.
> What the characters want.
> What makes life tough for the characters...then what makes it tougher.

What forces the characters to change.

What the author chooses to end the book with.

A good handy man continually collects odd screws and bolts. When writers read, they collect the screws and bolts of story construction. Then when they write, their unconscious has a stockpile from which to select. That's the way it works.

TAKE IT FOR A SPIN

Challenge yourself to read three stories a week and to find the nine items we've listed. You will begin to admire the work of many authors.

Next challenge yourself to choose one of the story paradigms described in this section. Having chosen it, use it to spin a tale. Step by step. Don't worry if the tale is good or not. Just keep spinning it using the paradigm you have chosen as your prompter.

After you have spun a tale, work on writing it out in a fuller version. Begin by going down the list of items we have suggested you look for in stories you read. Decide what your choices will be for your story.

Write from the beginning to the end. It is important to story writing to finish stories. If you have finished a story, even if it is not in the final form it will take, you know you can do it.

You have written a version with a beginning, middle and end. That is an accomplishment.

If you think you will write a perfect beginning before you get to the middle and a perfect middle before you get to the end, you run the risk of never finishing. You run the risk of forever telling yourself you can't do it well enough. Doing it well enough means writing a version from beginning to end. Then you know you can do it, and if you've done it once, you can do it again as often as your new ideas and revisions require. Make a whole story, then tinker with the parts. You may have to change the ending if you tinker with the beginning, but at least you have something to work on! Having a whole piece of work to tinker with means a writer is more likely to finish the work just as having a canvas means a painter is more likely to make a painting than if he were without one!

chapter eight

Raspberry Picking:
How can writers use readers' responses to refine their perceptions of their own writing?

AUGUST 11

Dear Sheila,

We went raspberry picking. Annie Rose, my 2½-year-old, was tired of it all after about twenty minutes of picking. "Home" she kept saying, whining, crying. What made it worse for her is that she dislikes raspberries. When we picked strawberries later, guess who led the way? In any case, after more imploring to her unhearing, totally absorbed raspberry-loving parents and sister, she planted her foot squarely into the flat of berries. JOLT! I was upset at first, then incredulous, then I laughed with my husband as we sorted the squished little rubies from the flat and left. Annie Rose jolted us out of our picking frenzy, our concentrated tornado of task.

Jolts are precious things. They enable me to think about something differently, and that's hard to do when a person's as stubborn as I can be some times.

Replanted, looking at
a clear blue sky,
Christi

August 15

Dear Christi,

I'm in Vancouver, B.C., on the 28th floor of the Blue Horizon Hotel on Robson Street. The sun is shining and I look out over English Bay: a tugboat in the water is like a hat; from this height, a marina filled with sailboats looks like a page of Chinese characters; the mountains in the distance are like a hippopotamus; seaplanes are like dragonflies; rooftops are like empty streets; fir trees are like thimbles; my balcony is like a postage stamp; clouds in the sky are like the inside of a quilt; cars on a highway are like parts on a conveyer belt; a child's foot in a flat of raspberries is like a mushroom sprouting in the garden!

What a story about Annie Rose! How direct we all once were as children. The jolt you were open to reminds me of what happens to me every time I revise a piece of writing. I

Writing In A Convertible With The Top Down

write in a task of getting the words on paper and then I look at them and they are not as beautiful, as streamlined, as rich and full and lyrical as I hoped, as I know is possible.

We must come to know the size, shape, taste, sound, smell, and texture of the real work buried inside the task, the pleasure of the berries apart from the interminable picking.

I am enclosing a poem of mine, recently accepted for publication and an earlier "task" version. I am grateful for them both—grateful for the early version because while doing it, I sat with my notebook recording images and details from my surroundings. I am grateful for the later version because it is smoother, more informed by the emotional truth of the moment, more elegantly constructed. It evokes the berries and not the work of picking them.

How did I move from the first to the last? Readers in my writing workshop read the first one and their responses were the "little Annie Rose with her foot in the raspberry flat" for me. I was "jolted" into realizing their emotions were not engaged. I felt each word until I was able to choose the ones that best described the other person in the poem at the time I was evoking. Then I could discover what my emotion was at the time I was inspired to write. The revision from then on stayed more focused, coming from emotion and observation of the time and place. That kind of writing engages readers. Here is my "task" version first and then my rewrite.

FIRE HEAD
AND TWO ORANGE WINGS OVER
THE HORIZON

South of Monterey we pull off the road
onto a lay by over the blue Pacific,
watch the sun burn a hole
in the sky and the sky like flesh
turn grey around such fire.

When you nap, I pick up my notebook,
notice your shorts, wet from the river,
show through the jeans you drive in.
The sun burns more discriminate over a thin
haze of purple, my eyes fastening the glow
in spots on the pages. As I write, a constant
wind moves the dune grass into flames
like the sunlight I saw reflected
on the canyon walls today as we swam.
Now orange spreads from the sun
and I stare longer. The wings drop
behind clouds leaving only the furry
golden head of a butterfly. You wake,
kiss me, see the monarch spread its color
in thin salt air and for a few moments

*we barely have to look harder at all
to see the eternal flames, the grass,
the canyon walls on fire.*

THE COASTAL ROUTE, AFTER ARGUING

*As we drive, I see wind
moving the dune grass
like flames on the hillsides.*

*This is how river light
looked as I watched canyon walls
today, you diving upstream.*

*I'd hollered that great noise
between us again, mountain tops
of stone pulverized in air,
you like an unaware camper
caught in dark, descending ash.*

*Now before dusk, the sun burns
a hole in the sky and the sky
turns grey around that wound.*

For a moment, we look at the sunset,
open wings of a monarch
spread behind clouds.

>Yours in writing the strong stuff
that comes after the jolt,
Sheila

A KEY: UNHUNCH AND LOOK AT WHAT YOU'RE DOING

Have you ever noticed how your ears hear differently with somebody else listening? How you might at first hunch your shoulders to your ears in defiance that anything must change? Unhunch and look at what you're doing means getting out of the insular world of your own mind and feelings and seeing how and where you are making contact with an audience.

TAKE IT FOR A SPIN

Ask someone to read your work to you. Read it to them. Record the work and listen to it with someone. The feeling in the writing becomes clearer when you listen with extra ears.

Even if you are going to have verbal response from your listener or peer editor, do this exercise first. You will get a body experience, a registering with yourself of where your writing works and where it hasn't fully evoked your experience yet.

When you go back to your work, you will remember the sound of the jarring sentences and the inspired ones. You will know better how to guide yourself.

To document the moment, write about how it felt and what you noticed when you listened to your work. Be detailed. What in your writing was jarring, what was smooth, what was touching, what perked interest, what was flat, what was obtuse? Where did you feel the sensations about this in your own body? How were those sensations like other times in your life? For instance, if you read the words and felt a kind of hollowness was that like when you say the "wrong thing" to a friend or a partner? When you felt the sound of your words sounding just right, did it seem like the air around you was suddenly cleansed like after a thunderstorm?

chapter nine

The Dentist:
How do we create a good climate for strong growing?

August 18

Dear Sheila,

Last week I had some terrifying dental work done—a skin graft. A piece of skin was cut from my palate and stitched to the receding gum below my front lower incisors. And today, a mere seven days after the deed, I am all but healed.

A story is like a gash in the mouth—the skin will form and heal only if the mouth is kept closed and protected and nurtured.

Start writing something. Feel it out. Keep it to yourself.

Mum's the word,
Christi

August 21

Dear Christi,

How important to remember not only the word "closed" but also the word "nurtured." How can we nurture the stories growing inside us until we are ready to share our drafts? I think the answer is establishing *climate*. We can create and maintain the right climate for story growing.

Here are some ideas:

1. I read lots of stories with friends and instead of analyzing the plot and theme, we just repeat the details, images and phrases that strike us. I saw this demonstrated in a workshop by Natalie Goldberg, author of *Writing Down the Bones*. We keep at this until there is nothing more to add. This elicits appreciation for how quickly, durably, and lastingly writing affects us. I can also do this activity in my journal, or I can talk aloud to myself after reading.
2. I have a writing group. We pose questions taken from the moment. Why are the birds lined up on the telephone wire just now? Where is the lady who is walking past going? Why? Who will miss her or be waiting? What does she think about the number of dandelions in the lawn? Everyone writes their own answers. Each person reads their responses to the questions. We listen with our inner ears to the liveliness as everyone enjoys the various answers. Working without a group, I can promise myself I will ask a question in the morning and answer it in the

evening. I must ask questions I couldn't possibly know the answer to. What is important is what I make up.

3. I practice the "yes and" game I learned in acting classes. Everyone stands or sits in a circle. One person starts off a story with a phrase—perhaps "Once upon a time a letter fell from the mailman's big bag." Another continues "and...." Most of us are used to a "yes, but" approach which is editorial and limiting. We need to celebrate in order to write. We need to acknowledge and to accept. We need to say "yes and" to keep going, to grow a story. If you can't find a group, do this yourself challenging yourself to keep going, "Yes, and..."

Yours in incubation,
Sheila

August 21

Dear Sheila,

Beginnings are the hardest. I rewrite them thousands of times, yet every time I start a book, I feel this need to think, "*This is it* I'm writing the first chapter. Here it is."

Then I get nervous and tell myself stuff like, "Relax, already, Christi. This doesn't have to be the Great American Novel. You don't have to change the world here." But always I return to the thought, "You are the storyteller of the day. Be yourself and start talking." It helps me sometimes to turn the brightness control on my computer monitor down all the way; I still type, and the words still go into the machine; I just can't see it happening. I feel more like I am talking, and I worry less about the horror of my beginnings.

Here are the beginning pages of the story I'm starting. It's a little scary to send this to you, not because I'm ashamed, but because it feels too solid then, too permanent. As if by sending it to you, it's published. Actually, it is published in a way, since my definition of publication is sharing. But I'm sharing this with you as the beginning of a beginning. That's all. Nothing really big.

THE ANIMAL IN ME
BY CHRISTI KILLIEN

"You're just like your father."

The words pierced Robin's heart like poison darts, their venom spreading quickly through his entire body and making him sick. "What do you know?" he said to his stepsister, Irene. It was the start of one of their hate sessions. Robin hated the hate sessions, but he felt trapped, sucked into them by his own anger. He always left them feeling as if he needed to shed a skin, like a snake.

"I know plenty," Irene said, drying a dish Robin had handed to her. "I've lived with you both for two years now, God help me." Irene was fourteen, Robin twelve. His natural mother had died when Robin was five, from cancer, and then five years later Robin's father had married Irene's mother, Sher.

Robin said nothing, as usual. He wasn't a sharp talker, like Irene. She generally massacred him verbally He handed her another plate.

"Oh, you're the perfect little goody-goody at school, a regular angel boy," she sniped. "Sixth grade star, big deal. Wait 'till you get to junior high when you're not such hot spit. Then everyone'll see what a dork you really are."

"What did I do?" Robin asked.

"You *wouldn't* know," said Irene.

"What's the matter with you, anyway?" Robin finally blurted. "Got your period?" He knew it was mean the minute he said it, but it was a hate session, right?

"Shut up!" Irene splashed water at Robin's glasses and he reached up and wiped the suds off his lenses with the back of his wrist.

"*You* shut up!" he shouted.

Irene's face burned red. She went back to drying. "God, I can't believe I'm stuck here with such a dweeb of a brother." She shook her head, her short dark hair swinging around her cheeks. She had just gotten it cut that afternoon. When Robin had seen her, he had laughed. Well, actually he had laughed and said, "Playing with the lawn mower again, huh Irene?" Was that what had made her so mad? Robin wondered now.

Who cares what made her mad, he thought, shoving the next dish into her hand. She shouldn't be so touchy. So mean. She was just like her mother. Robin's arms jittered with fury. He wanted to kill her, he really did. His stepmother, Sher, called it sibling rivalry. There is no such thing as sibling rivalry, Robin was thinking. It was just a fancy name for hate. Pure, unadulterated despising for someone.

Well, it's very different from what I'd "planned"—where did this sibling stuff come from? The paragraphs feel harsh to me right now, but I'm going to keep going on it, for a while anyway.

Full of surprises,
Christi

August 24

Dear Christi,

Irene and Robin are both identifiable figures and my sympathy for Robin is aroused right off the bat because he asks

Writing In A Convertible With The Top Down

questions despite the fact that he does cover up the time for answers by plunging ahead anyway into the "hate session." How we warm to our mechanical habits of emotion and thought!

I love the image of you sitting before the darkened computer screen typing away and not looking at what words are appearing. I think that is great advice for anyone writing! When we invent our material we need to feel free and that means free of what we think of what we are writing.

Peter Elbow, author of several books on teaching writing, talks a lot about a ten-minute writing exercise for writers. He says you set a timer and then just write or type sentences without stopping for ten minutes. That's the whole thing—it is the "without stopping" part that is hard for some of us to let ourselves do.

Just like musicians play scales, and dancers do warm up steps, and athletes do drills, so writers can do the ten minute free write. We must warm to our tasks, train our bodies, overcome simple inertia, get going.

No time for chewing on erasures or even for erasing! Just scratch out a word that bothers you but keep the writing implement moving! And no time for clock watching. Keep writing.

"What if I run out of things to say?" The answer is just keep writing the same sentence over and over even if it's, "I don't have anything to say. I can't think of anything to say." After all, the only goal here is to keep writing in sentences for ten minutes.

So I set the timer and "Go" until the timer buzzes meaning "Stop." I finish the sentence I am working on and shake my hands out. Whew, cramps in my fingers.

Did I ever really write the same thing over and over? Would I really bore myself for ten minutes? Mostly, I'm surprised by things I hardly knew were in my mind.

I share the writing if I feel secure and certain that there will be no criticism forthcoming. I like to use the Natalie Goldberg activity I wrote about to you where listeners merely say back the images, details and facts they heard from the writer. I am nourished as a writer when I learn that what I wrote leaves an impression.

So about *The Animal in Me*, "hate sessions," "just like your mother," "just like your father," "goody-goody," "splashed water at Robin's glasses," a haircut that made her look like she "was playing with the lawn mower again," "pure unadulterated despising for someone." Makes my skin prickle with goose bumps!

Toasting wonderful
beginnings,
Sheila

A KEY: RELAX, DON'T THINK ABOUT IT, IT WON'T SEEM SO SCARY

"Relax, don't think about it, it won't seem so scary" is easier said than done. Somehow, we feel that even in the privacy of our own beginnings, to put words and sentences on paper or on a computer screen, which resembles paper, is too concrete a reminder that we may be terrible at writing. Nobody likes to look failure in the face. Easier to talk to people and let the words drift over the air waves away from us than to write, face to face with the words.

Writers must begin to believe that the words are not going to solidify. In beginnings we find treasures and we find what must be carved away. If we make a mistake in judgment about that, we only need a new sheet of paper or our delete key. We have wasted very little. They value of beginnings is that we begin, that we once again get into the movement of making our words have a life outside of our minds. Here's one way to go about this:

TAKE IT FOR A SPIN

Write "throw away pages." Write them to something or someone who will not talk back to you. Sounds silly but it works.

Write to your blanket from childhood. Write to the goal posts on your favorite field. Write to the street light you wait at every morning, or write to the forsythia bush in your neighbor's yard. The forsythia bush has many things to think about—the sun, the rain, the temperature. We don't expect it to think long and hard about our writing attempts.

Go ahead and address yourself to something out there.

Wasn't it freeing to unload and not worry about where you were going with it? Beginnings can be like that. It is profitable to respect your own interest and your strong feeling.

What in the writing practice you just finished is most interesting or surprising to you? Continue with that as your focus. Let yourself write without that deadly fear of future structure.

chapter ten

Airports, Nursing Homes, and Cafés: How do writers keep their writing from being boring?

AUGUST 28

Dear Christi,

    I'm at the gate for Southwest Airlines flight 832 with one half hour till flight time. My fifteen-year-old daughter is next to me absorbed in the "Cosby Show" on the TV in the waiting area. There's a boy nearby, about 12 years old, string bean tall and handsome, whose grandma keeps clucking at how big his feet have gotten, how manly they look in his new white athletic shoes. On the floor in front of the TV's orange cabinet sit what my generation called the peanut gallery—little kids who watched the *Howdy Doody Show*. To this day, Clarabell is a character I remember, the one who didn't speak, the one who swept out an old, silent attic and waited for imaginary friends to fill the space.

How odd to end today with television. I've been to the desert—the air like air in a sauna, the orange brown dirt roads, men with arms the color of clay, roadrunners in our path, magpies whirling skyward here and there from yucca plants, the mockingbirds and gold finches, jack rabbits whose ears were so tall I thought at first there were deer in the sagebrush. It's quiet where I was and clean. I loved the sun, so bright it gives the air a yellow aura, and the lovely flatness before Red Mountain, Black Mountain, the buttes and the Florida (Flor-ee-da) ranges, tinted purple and jagged in the distance.

I was 97 miles from El Paso in New Mexico near a town formed when the Topeka Railroad met the Santa Fe. The companies chose to call the town by the name of a long time employee named Mr. Deming.

My father bought a half acre of Deming desert in the '60's. Once I told him I liked New Mexico and he gave me his half acre with many reminders that it was worthless. But I like land that's worthless. That way it's land. It's what it is and not what someone thinks it should be.

Thinking this way, I want to tell anyone who wishes to write to find a piece of "worthless" land—some corner off a sidewalk along a long forgotten lot, the neglected strip between two buildings, a gully in a park, whatever they can find that seems ignored. They must stand as close as they can to it, see the view from there, listen to the sounds they hear in that place, smell all that's in the air. They will learn to drink in through the senses.

But there is more: A state park ranger outside Deming told me about the way kids will catch a baby mocking bird, cage it for a time and keep it fed. When let free, the bird will stay around the child's house, flying and whistling, homesteading where it was taken. That's how I feel about this land. I was taken to it by surprise, and it fed me, land silent as Clarabell's attic. In my memory, I homestead there, honoring the part of me my senses set free.

Yours from the dry heat,
Sheila

August 29

Dear Sheila,

I've just returned from my trip to Helena, Montana and the specter of my grandfather in a nursing home.

On a happier occasion, I was in Helena ten years ago, in February of 1979, when we experienced a full eclipse. Astronomers and physicists came from all over the world to view it from Helena. Total darkness for twenty minutes or so. The street lights came on. Very few people were left unmoved by the experience. Seeing ourselves outlined right there on the moon. That's our shadow up there! We are on a planet, we are round, we are real.

But there is another definition of eclipse: missing the point. So many of my grandmother's friends love to tell stories, but only a few do it well. Why is this? "Get to the point!" I wanted to scream many times. My mother just stopped listening to the storytelling and fell asleep. I persevered. And then, after fifteen minutes of lead-in, of telling what was eaten and the routes taken and decisions made, the storyteller said, "She was in a car accident and her baby was thrown from the window, but both are okay." ARG! I almost missed it, and my mother missed it for sure. When are details delicious and when are they tedious? When do they enrich the story? When do they bog it down and eclipse the thrust of the story?

I clipped an article from the *Seattle Times* several years ago entitled, "Research uncovers trivial facts: Bores are an acute social disease." The word bore is harsh, I realize, but since I can scarcely bear to look at my latest, still unpublished book again, I include myself in the category. We are all boring sometimes. Mark Leary, the psychologist doing this study, agrees.

Students in the studies he conducted suggested 210 tiresome things other people do, which the researchers distilled into 43 themes for a second survey of 297 students. They used a "boringness index," and concluded that "chronically and excessively boring persons" were not reporting their own feelings and attitudes and opinions as much as the less boring people were, and that they made fewer statements of fact.

Instead, their conversation included complaints about themselves, trivialities and talk about superficial things, showing interest in only one topic, and utterances like "Uh-huh."

Oh, to be intensely interesting and relevant all the time. To have that exquisite, skull-expanding relatedness every time I open my mouth or take pen in hand!

Is there a vitamin for this?
Christi

August 31

Dear Christi,

I'm at Cody's Bookstore Café in Berkeley. Twenty years ago today I was marrying my first husband, the father of my children. Ten years ago I was separated from him. My then almost four-year-old son and almost six-year-old daughter named the little house I sublet for the summer the Poetry House because, with three published poems under my belt, I was writing in earnest, applying to the University of Washington's Graduate School of Creative Writing. My son said if he were big enough, he would build a boat and "run it" while I sat in the cabin writing and writing.

"We are round; we are real." How suddenly real I felt, the shape of my new life on the faces of my two children. What a blessing that their essences knew mine. That is what tided us over the difficulties of joint custody, their going back and forth between two homes, their loneliness yearning for an unnameable unity now that their parents' marriage was over.

Our life, though, had range. We had no mold we had to fit into, no status quo to keep. My son pursued trumpet, ceramics, soccer, wood working, drafting, sailing and windsurfing. My daughter went for gymnastics, piano, French, "Knowledge Bowl" at school and being a counselor at YMCA camp. They have "run" a boat for me to write on by captaining their own lives.

Here at the café with tables so close together they seem like one table, I can't help eavesdropping on a young gay man who is counseling a young woman after the suicide of her lover. A lover of his once killed himself. Overcoming guilt feelings, he has learned how deeply responsible we all are for our own lives, how easily parents and children look to each other for life validation, how chokingly we hold on to each other when we insist on their lives giving ours meaning and how we choke ourselves for someone else's benefit. She sobs now in his arms, then suddenly stops sobbing and speaks again in a rush of words about her lover's family, their religion.

Christi, what do I think makes someone or someone's writing boring? Lack of essential self, lack of connection between self and the environment one finds oneself in, lack of associations between that environment and the part of the self for which it serves as a "reminding factor" (a term Kathryn Holme coins in her autobiography *Undiscovered Country*).

Writing In A Convertible With The Top Down

When I want to remember, I use a clustering technique (the name for a writing activity described in *Writing the Natural Way* by Gabriele Lusser Rico).

I take an object in the room in which I am sitting. I write down what it is called in the center of a blank page. Then I shoot off the names of places where I have seen a similar object:

- **Blue candles made of honeycomb**
  - Bumpy texture of the netting on a recital tutu—I am 7, my sister 5 ½ / I am
  - Black & white hexagon-shaped tiles on grandma's bathroom floor. If I stare at them, they rise several feet.
  - I am 2, 3, 4, 5, 6, 7, 8, 9, 10, 11, 12, 13, 14, 15, 16. Why did birthday cakes stop at 16?
  - The color of sky as I saw it from Rockaway Beach
  - White wick like a birthday candle
  - Green waves licking the skyline

After awhile I get the feeling that one of these is very interesting to write about. I write about it for ten minutes without censoring my thoughts or stopping. Let me show you. I'll start in the room I sit in now, wind back to the past, and if I want, wind back to the present:

> I sit now in a café. I stare at two blue candles made of honeycomb. Blue was always my favorite color and pink was always my sister's favorite. Was

that true or did we make it up in order to make things easy when people gave us gifts or asked us to choose?

My sister and I in so many pictures before the breakfront, a piece of French Provincial styled furniture my mother's mother bought for her and for each of her sisters. It moved when we moved from one side of Union, New Jersey, to the other and to Willmette, Illinois, and back again to Union.

But the picture I am thinking of today was taken in front of it when it was very new to us. I am 7 and my sister 5½. We are dressed in tutus for a dance recital, rouge on our cheeks and flowers in our hair. I am taller than she is as I won't be after age 12. I am a better ballet student my mother tells me. She says I am more able to make friends. I am conscientious. I must take care of my sister. What a big skirt to fill and my tutu is no longer than hers.

We are all born to stories. When we pay attention to our essential selves we can't be boring. Writing is a boat we design, make seaworthy, and steer to keep our character alive and well.

Yours on the high seas,

Sheila

A KEY: LINK TO THE LANDSCAPE

Link to the landscape means immerse yourself in a landscape and its people and they will feed you with images, bits of conversation, remembered events, everything you need to write with fresh images. One thing that gets in the way of us allowing ourselves to experience what is out there is the number of clichés we are accustomed to hearing and using without thinking. We may experience the landscape as nothing special because we can't see past the "Oh, isn't this pretty?" and the "Oh, wouldn't Aunt Dorothy love this" and the "Having a great time, wish you were here" language that clogs our minds.

TAKE IT FOR A SPIN

Clichés are overused words and phrases that have lost their connection to experience. They are words the brain interprets but not the heart. "Having a great time" means everything's cool, but it doesn't relate experience that can be enjoyed through the senses, or experience that evokes the very nature of where one is, both physically and emotionally.

Here is a list of clichés you have probably heard:

> Don't talk about religion or politics.
> Don't feed the animals.

Don't kiss him/her on the first date.
Ladies don't cross their legs.
Keep your elbows off the table.
Keep your feet off the furniture.
You deserve a break today.
Reach out and touch someone.
Cross that bridge when you come to it.
Eat three bites of everything on your plate.
Be quiet/ Simmer down/ Hold your horses.

With this kind of chatter constantly in our minds we have to do something to free ourselves from it before we can make more truthful contact with our subjects. One way to free ourselves from the power clichés have to keep us from experiencing is to play with them. Put an individual in the situation described by one of the clichés above and the situation becomes specific and interesting. The cliché is defeated.

For instance:

Albert Strong always kisses on the first date, but only the date's fingertips.
Elsie Leland is on a diet; she eats one bite in the morning, one at noon, and one before she goes to bed.

> John Chalmers keeps his feet off the furniture; every
> night he puts his prosthetic leg in the closet.
> Andy knows how to reach out and touch someone.
> He is the orangutan at our zoo and yesterday
> he grabbed a little girl who was licking an ice
> cream cone.

Try your hand at defeating the clichés that swim around in your head. Go to a location. Jot down as many clichés as you can think of. Then take some of them and insert an individual who can make the cliché unique. If the individual becomes really interesting to you, keep writing about him or her:

To practice speaking from yourself and staying interesting, you may want to try a cluster. Clustering helps you remember what is special to your experience. Look back at Sheila's letter from Berkeley. Go to a place you can sit and write. Make a cluster by using images from where you sit. Let yourself record images from your past that you associate with what you notice where you sit. Suddenly, you will feel ready to write. The writing you do will evoke you in a particular time and place.

chapter eleven

Highway Patrol: How do we help each other as writing partners?

September 11

Dear Sheila,

The fighting stepsiblings, Irene and Robin, have turned into five girls on a Bainbridge Island baseball team.

As I write this first draft, I feel like a hungry animal, clawing and pacing and snatching at bits of meat. I am a tiger and this is life and death.

I steal. Yes, I really do. When I get stuck, I open one of my favorite author's books and look for a good line. When I see it, I snatch it and plug it into my narrative. I rip the line up a bit so it fits my situation, but so much the better. No one will recognize the corpse later.

I think of the other beasts out there trying for my prey. That lady out in California who has this same story idea. I'll get to it first.

I use my instincts. My nose is to the ground as I write, sniffing the story and the characters. Sometimes my mouth salivates at the odor. Other times, when I smell something rotten, or even get a hint of the rancid, I stop. Hmmm. Danger here. Change it. Re-evaluate, but quickly. Time is of the essence. The prey will escape. I've learned to trust my instincts so that if something even occurs to me, I know it's right.

If someone looks at me wrong, I snarl, I *roar*. Out of my way! I'm stalking this story and I'm loving it, but get out of my forest so I can see that little rabbit when it twitches. I'm going to pounce on it, and it won't be a pretty sight.

Fiercely,
Christi

SEPTEMBER 17
Dear Christi,

"Sulking," "roaring," "snarling," "beasts...trying for...prey." This is you, a lively, directed writer in the thick of her forest and her body, using all of her powers to get what she is after.

I like to use the power of my senses in my writing. A poem by Pablo Neruda once inspired me.

THE QUEEN

I have named you queen.
There are taller ones than you, taller.
There are purer ones than you, purer.
There are lovelier than you, lovelier.

But you are the queen.

When you go through the streets
no one recognizes you.
No one sees your crystal crown, no one looks
at the carpet of red gold
that you tread as you pass,
the nonexistent carpet.
And when you appear
all the rivers sound
in my body, bells
shake the sky,
and a hymn fills the world.
Only you and I,
only you and I, my love,
listen to it.

Neruda thinks of all that he sees that no one else sees and all that happens inside him as his queen passes. And what he sees and feels are real details that come in through the senses, in this case, of sight and sound. And coming in, the images take on a life. She is the queen!

What I do—and have shared with other writers—is think of someone I have strong feelings about, either of love or dislike. Then I think of something to call that person: I call you rocking chair, I call you book, I call you column, I call you sea. Then I copy Neruda, his second and third stanzas. I write the characteristics no one else sees in that person that have made me name them what I did.

Next I focus inside myself: what happens in me when I see this rocking chair, that book, column or sea?

Christy Buckly, a student of mine many years ago in a Saturday morning creative writing class, used this idea and wrote:

I NAME YOU BOOK

Nobody knows you have an endless
amount of pages.
Nobody knows under that cover
is a full world.
Whenever you are around,
I turn poised.
I try to change you,
not knowing when I do,
I am ripping out a page.

See you there, Christi, where the instinctive animal in us takes over and rejoices in the hunt. *Mazel Tov* (Yiddish for good luck)!

Naming myself writer,
No one sees the words flowing
from my pen, how quickly my
hand records what I see, touch,
taste, hear and smell. But when
I come near myself all the pages
are filled,
Sheila

S<small>EPTEMBER</small> 20

Dear Sheila,

I NAME YOU HIGHWAY PATROLMAN

When you say "No, it can't be done,"
No one suspects your desire
No one sees the scared boy as the
tornado rips down the road.

When you stop my frenzied juggling
I dump the twenty balls in despair,
Not knowing when I do,
I'm piercing you with a patrolman's badge.

This poem is about me and my husband Bill. When I get in the highly creative phase of writing a first draft, creative energy bubbles out of me and soaks into every aspect of my life. Just driving to Bellevue this morning, I wrote down five ideas on Post-its stuck to my steering wheel—an idea for a short chapter book entitled *The Bike Rodeo*; the vision of a long, cotton purple skirt I want to make; a better name for a character in the book I'm writing now; an image for one of the bike tricksters in my first idea; and, finally, a new design for the kitchen of the house I started designing on Saturday! Add this to wanting to paint Molly's and Annie Rose's bedrooms and the fleeting desire to apply for the part-time teaching job open at Bill's school and you get an idea of what I've been like to live with lately.

I am a crazed woman in a swirling purple skirt flying across the Lake Washington Bridge while conducting a Bach Suite. Bill is overwhelmed. He is sapped of his own creative energy trying to absorb all my changes.

I have the characters, I have a plot, but my initial vision of a fifth-grade comedy about bras and baseball—the working title was *Wednesday Is Bra Day*—has turned into the story of five girls not ready for the womanhood being pressed on them. The new title is *The Daffodils*.

It is more serious, although there is still humor. And horror of horrors, the single third-person viewpoint won't cut it! The story requires the viewpoints of all five girls, something I've never done before, not to mention the fact that most children's book how-to's say to stick to one viewpoint. So what. I don't care about rule books. I'm rewriting, rereading, rethinking and discovering what this book is to be about.

Focusing on one hole
in the Swiss cheese,
Christi

September 26

Dear Christi,

The library grows more important to me with the days getting shorter. When the evening comes early I like to sit and read. Fall and I can almost feel myself as a young girl walking home from school to the familiar smells and sounds of home. The electric lights' glow against dusk outside our window, the nubby upholstery on the old couch itching behind my knees, the doughy balls I'd roll in front of the TV from soft white Wonder Bread slices.

I can smell one of my mother's casseroles baking. I can hear the water running for the hot bath I'd sometimes take even before dinner when my father, a pharmaceutical salesman, was "on the road" and my mom and sister and I grew more informal. I feel the soft long flannel nightgown I wore, the huge and fluffy slippers.

I see myself at a narrow desk, the drop leaf kind with no room for your elbows once a pad and books are on it. I am struggling with a play my third grade teacher asked me to write.

Another flash and I'm doing geometry waiting for the phone to ring. I feel myself dashing out of my room and into my mother's room to answer the one extension we had upstairs. A date! Another flash and I am looking sadly out the living room window through the dusk to the other side of the street where a boy and his family are moving, their furniture almost all boarded into a truck. I feel the wish that he had liked me, a girl.

If even our memories are like this—let through one impression like the smell of fall air and things to see, taste, touch, smell and hear pop out of nowhere—why should we expect our creative energy to know any bounds?

The image of you behind your dashboard covered with Post-its! I picture them like little pink petals, as if the angels had been there casting those petals before you so your journey would be rich in beauty.

But a journey does require focus. Your "I Name You" effort has me wanting to talk about this. In the first stanza, we are focused on the highway patrolman, his desire. For what? Can we have images here? Perhaps more lines about specific things he desires and the highway patrolman's nature. I love the last two lines: No one sees the scared boy as the/tornado rips down the road.

The next stanza shifts to you, the speaker, as Pablo Neruda does, but with a difference—you tell us the highway patrolman actually does something to you (stops your juggling) rather than what happens to you when you are near him or what you

WRITING IN A CONVERTIBLE WITH THE TOP DOWN

do when you see him. Also, juggling is not the kind of thing a highway patrolman usually stops. I can see the highway patrolman directing others when a tornado is in the area and being scared himself, but it is hard to get the juggling balls into the same landscape.

Then when the juggler (the speaker) drops the balls she thinks she is piercing the highway patrolman with his badge. This is a hard thing to imagine happening in the real world—that a juggler would be juggling when a tornado is coming, that dropping balls actually causes a badge to pierce a man. So we have a few too many landscapes flooding into the stanzas: highway patrol, tornado, juggler. Or we are as of yet without the unifying fabric that would allow all these images to work in one context.

What would happen if you expanded the first stanza to keep your eye on the highway patrolman? If you said all that you see in images so specific that they evoke the "desire" you sense is in the man? Then, when you move to the interior, say what you see and feel in yourself. Make sure you stick with yourself in the situation of being stopped by a highway patrolman. Remember in line one he says, "No, it can't be done."

I think following this tack you will evoke much more of what it feels like to be in the state of chaotic, generative energy and have a partner with whom to contend. I look forward to a next version.

A woman in a swirling purple skirt who can fly over Lake Washington while conducting a Bach Suite inspires the rest of us to take stock. If we can fly, why are we walking?

Sitting on the same
wedge of cheese with you,
Sheila

OCTOBER 2

Dear Sheila,

I finished the first draft of *The Daffodils* this weekend! I write fast once I get started. BRAG!

I'm excited about this book. I think it's the best thing I've ever done. The multiple viewpoints work well, I love the way the idea of community comes in at the end to pull these five girls together, I like the metaphor of fifth grade girls forced into bloom like daffodil bulbs before their natural time. It works and I'm proud of it! Has anybody else but me read it, you ask? No! But if I don't love the thing I don't think anyone else will.

It's funny how a book evolves. I started with *Wednesday Is Bra Day*, the idea coming from a friend's comment to her ten-year-old daughter who wanted a bra, and wanted to wear it to school. And now the book has nothing of this except the initial scene, where an eleven-year-old wants a bra.

I think of a story I once heard. I have no idea of the source, and I'm probably massacring it in this retelling, but it fits so well what I'm describing. A husband bought his wife a beautiful vase for her birthday. She loved it and put it in a place of prominence in the living room. Soon, however, it became obvious that the room was simply not grand enough for the vase. So the husband offered to build a separate room for it. The building began, and as the days passed, the plans for the room grew to include an entire new house. But even that was not grand enough. In the end, a glorious castle had been erected with a place of honor for the vase. When the vase was brought in, however, it was clear that it no longer fit. The castle the vase had inspired had outgrown the vase so completely that the vase wasn't appropriate any longer. It was given away.

There are a few tiny places in my castle that I have mental question marks next to, and I'm very willing and interested in hearing responses from my writer's group, but for now, it is wonderful. I trust my group to be gentle and honest with me, and I know that I don't have to do what they say.

It took me a while to get to this point, and our group has struggled together to get this sense of safety. But it is worth it. If there are flaws, they'll help me with them. And I thank them.

As I'm thanking you right now for your comments about my Highway Patrolman poem. You are a gentle, thoughtful critiquer, Sheila. I know you don't like the word critique—since it comes from the same root as criticize. Perhaps responder is better. Your responses are very loving. I don't feel in any way crushed or even disappointed. Really. You are right. And I've revised!

I NAME YOU HIGHWAY PATROLMAN

When you say, "No, it can't be done,"
No one suspects your desire.
Even as you patrol in your uniform,
you think of English gardens, hollyhocks
And travel to Kenya.
No one sees the scared little boy as the
tornado rips down the road.

I ask for permission to go on.
The whirl dies, the road is a tomb,
Empty, still, dreary.
You feel it, too. Next time I'll smile and wave,
and keep going.

As Annie Rose says when she is creating, "I'm *making*!"

                                                                 Christi

OCTOBER 12
Hi Christi,

    Thank you for the compliment about being gentle and thoughtful. I like thinking about writing. I like wondering where a particular piece may want to be going. I like monitoring my own internal emotional response line by line.

Writing In A Convertible With The Top Down

Creators need response, audience, sympathetic ears. But responding should never be confused with fixing. Sometimes you may act as an editor seeing exactly what needs changing or shortening for the piece to be stronger, but you must wait either until the trust level is very high between you and the writer or the writer has written so much that the piece teeters on the verge of crystallization and your editorial remarks are like a light sun shower refreshing the air. Before those times, and if the responder is not skilled enough to be an editor, the responder must stick only to response and that is really enough to help a writer keep growing.

Your revision is exciting. The first five lines give me a very sharp image of the Highway Patrolman full of desire behind his role and uniform. The sixth line shows me another even more interior aspect of this person called Highway Patrolman.

The "I" comes in the second stanza asking to go on although a no was given in the poem's first line. When the "I" does go on, the road is still and dreary. The "I" knows Highway Patrolman feels this dreary tomblike quality also. I like this coming together.

Therefore, I have trouble with the next lines. Why in the circumstances of the poem with the "you" and the "I" brought together for a moment, would the "I" begin thinking about next time? Hang out on the dreary road a line or two. Don't be too quick to smile and wave.

I look forward to another revision. I think the piece is only a small step from full impact!

> Hearing the slap of tires
> over the roadway,
> Sheila

OCTOBER 15

Dear Sheila,

Grandpa died on October 4th, and I flew to Helena for his funeral. Teary-eyed after 58 years of marriage, Grandma said, "It was no bed of roses, Christi, but I'll miss him." He was 91. He had a full life. I bid him farewell, that box of ashes on the altar next to a picture of him as a dapper man in this thirties.

My aunt spoke eloquently of Grandpa's legacy—of the importance he placed on education since he had completed only the sixth grade, of his love of the outdoors and of his child-like sense of humor. But I remember how irritating his joking was to Grandma Milly. When feeling frisky and loaded, he would dance around the kitchen and sing this song:

> *Hell up a gump stump*
> *Harder than a bone*
> *Hair on Milly's hind-leg*
> *Long enough to comb!*

I can imitate this dance and song well, and everyone wanted me to do it again, as a tribute to Grandpa. I'm not going to sing Grandpa's song again because it was hurtful to Grandma, and it still is. That was part of the *no bed of roses*. So here you see I revise. I delete, I add, I change. The process of putting words and images together brings me closer to the center of myself, of the nitty gritty of me, and breaks me open to a world of gentleness and understanding that, sadly, I doubt my grandfather ever knew.

My writer's group responded to *The Daffodils* with wonderful encouragement and some specific problem areas that I feel need work, too. The first three chapters are a remnant of *Wednesday Is Bra Day*—the group said it was almost as if two books were stuck together. The one I want to write is chapter four to the end, so I picture the beginning again, write *again* about these five girls as I've come to know them.

Here is my poetry revision:

I NAME YOU HIGHWAY PATROLMAN

When you say "No, it can't be done,"
No one suspects your desire.
Even as you patrol in your uniform,
You think of English gardens, hollyhocks,
And travel to Kenya.

No one sees the scared little boy
As the tornado rips down the road.

I ask for permission to go on.
The whirl dies, the road is a tomb,
Empty, still, dreary.
I can see in your road-flat eyes
You feel it, too,
So I change your name.
You are blossom in the wind.

It occurs to me that maybe my grandpa was asked permission of too often. He wore a patrolman's badge for himself and everyone else. Well, now he is free!

May our trip to Yakima be free of highway patrolman, as well.

With love,
Christi

A KEY: RIP AND ROAR DOWN THE ROAD

As writers we have to roar and rip down the road, unhunched, driving our own route through all the seasons, staying relaxed so it won't be so scary, cooking for ourselves on the way from what we have on hand, sweetening it with metaphor. We recycle our inner life, eat the delicious fruit of other people's writing, build solid structures for our writing, and link to the landscape we are touring through. What independent, energetic, self sufficient, relentless, open, busy people writers are! And all of this in the seeming quiet of pen to paper or fingers to a keyboard.

Another oddity is that although in the end the writer is on a solitary journey, the writer is aided in ripping and roaring down the road by partnering up with trusted readers.

TAKE IT FOR A SPIN

Choose partners who are interested in writing. Ask a partner to write you a letter, telling about one place she's experienced at different times—the swimming pool in summer and then in winter or fall, the living room in the morning and then late afternoon, Hawaii when she was a teenager and then as a parent. Writing about the places at different times builds in a special reflective quality, gives the writing a turning point.

When you receive the writing, think of it as a work in progress:

> What is most interesting?
> Where do you think the writer backed away
>   from painful memories or new discovery?
> Where do you feel fulfilled, let down?
> What would you like the writer to talk more about?
> Where are you bored?

Where does the writer seem not to sound like herself?
What surprises did you really like?

Write a similar letter to your partner, including this list of questions for her to answer about your work. Read her responses and let those responses direct a new version. Keep up the correspondence and response until you each feel satisfied with your own writing. Then start in on a new piece from a new writing idea and exchange your versions for response.

By cultivating trusted readers you become a better reader of your own work as well as theirs.

chapter twelve

Porcupines:
How do we defend our creative process in the face of resistance?

A year after our last letters, just before the book hit the market, our editor called Christi and read this review to her:

> WRITING IN A CONVERTIBLE
> WITH THE TOP DOWN:
> A Unique Guide for Writers
> *Christi Killien and Sheila Bender*
>
> People looking for a book that teaches how to write excruciatingly bad prose need look no

further. Most of the authors' condescending advice takes the form of banal letters that sport cheery little closings like "Yours while the light is long, Sheila" and "Replanted, looking at the clear blue sky, Christi"—a tone more appropriate to Killien's children's books (*Putting on an Act*, etc.) than this allegedly adult title. Getting in touch with the creative self—"explor[ing] the cupboards of your memory"—seems to be more of a goal than producing readable prose. Poet and playwright Bender, viewing criticism with disdain, tells herself, "I must never listen to the words 'good' and 'bad.'" But since she later writes, "my friend once again, and once again not I," received an artist's grant, one might well question the shrewdness of her policy. A few writing exercises and comments on such matters as plot structure and character development appear amidst the anecdotes about berry picking and a beach holiday, but there are enough well-written guides to writing well that readers need not bother with this epistolary twaddle.

Christi called Sheila, but the phone wasn't enough. We needed to write to process our angst and in writing to one another again, we somehow set right, at least within ourselves, the injustice we felt had been done.

January 16

Dear Sheila,

A bad review. And not only a bad review, my worst nightmare come true. What is my reaction? When Tracy called two days ago and read it to me, at my request, I was stunned. Tracy laughed and said it was "so stupid." Then she waited. I had to have some response. I mumbled something about it being no big deal, the reviewer was obviously psychologically hooked here, most people I knew who bought writing books, myself included, didn't buy them based on a review, anyway.

I hung up feeling gutted. I'd been cool for Tracy, processed the review mentally, logically. Then I went to bed. Yesterday, I came home from dropping off the kids at school and day care and I slept. It was the immediate, deep, hiding kind.

That review knocked the wind out of me. I have wrestled with the differences between adult and children's novels. My old editor at Houghton Mifflin insists that my literary voice is humorous and that children's books is my genre. I hear the condescension in people's voices when I tell them I write children's books. "How special," I hear, just like the church lady on "Saturday Night Live." I am embarrassed.

I think about adult problems lately, about my three children, refinancing my mortgage, my relationship with my husband.

I'm 35 years old. Isn't it time to put away childish things and turn to the business of writing about adult lives?

Well, I've slipped into the cocktail party hoping that no one will notice I'm a children's book writer. Surely no one would be so rude as to make a scene of it, to point me out across the room, ask for my ID and then toss me out.

But, alas, it has happened.

My "tone," the reviewer says, is the offending element. My tone, as in, "I don't like your tone, Young Lady." We've stepped out of line here, Sheila. This is child-like, an embarrassment. It doesn't belong at the party.

Tone, style, voice—these all seem to me to mean the same thing, namely the projection onto paper of who I think I am. It is how I tell something and it is very revealing. I write from who I am, whether it is a children's novel, an adult novel or a letter. But for some reason, to this reviewer it is banal and condescending; it is not for adult readers. Do we see things too simply, Sheila? Or is that style threatening? Are we misfits in the complex adult world?

Having trouble defending myself,
Christi

JANUARY 19

Dear Christi,

Now that our book has gone through the editing for publication process, you may have forgotten that in our first draft, yours was the first letter. You ended that letter with a sign-off similar in feeling and function to the ones that close each of our letters now. Let me tell you something I never told you before: When I read the sign off, I heard a voice inside say, "Oh, no, that is a tone from way back when I was a kid." But then I wrote back to you, and signing off with a sincerely, or a love, or a yours, or a 'bye for now seemed wholly inadequate.

I thought, "Christi's onto something. This idea which I haven't explored since adolescence is fun. I am older now, more experienced. I wonder what my sign-offs will be each time I write. I wonder if I will be able to arrive at a phrase that encompasses the essence of what I have come to discover in my letters. Let me give it a try."

In finding the right sign offs to you, and in paying attention to yours, I expanded and grew larger in my feelings. And that is what we are advocating in our book—that writing is in its essence a generous act and although not all of what we put out on the page will "work" and much will be cut and reshaped, if we do not begin in an open, expanded, generous place inside ourselves toward ourselves, we may never get the work out to be shaped; we may never believe there is reason enough even to try.

In my opinion, the reviewer we are reacting to is not only ungenerous, but deceptive and manipulative. The question, my husband reminds me, with a book like ours is whether the process we talk about works. The reviewer doesn't seem to raise that question, notice the process, try it or report on its results.

Here is my letter to him.

Dear Unsigned,

You are completely comfortable dismissing trips to the beach and berry picking as banal. You are completely comfortable taking the authority to say a cheery tone is better reserved for children's books. And you take the authority to quote my words out of context in order to make it seem as if I am the one who is self-aggrandizing.

You write that I "disdain" criticism. I do not introduce the word "disdain" into my discussion. I say I don't listen to the words "good" and "bad" as I begin to write. I do not as a writer find it useful to listen to myself criticize myself as I write in the first stages. Perhaps, Unsigned, speaking for yourself, you might claim, "I start my writing each time by having a critic's voice inside me, a voice that indulges in faultfinding and censure, a voice that expresses judgments about the qualities and comparative worth of what I am doing." But you would not be among creative writers in this sentiment because creative writers know that voice is death to the spark they need.

Writing In A Convertible With The Top Down

You seem to think that since I report somewhere in letters that my "friend once again and once again not I received a $1000 grant" that I am less a writer and that my process doesn't serve me well. I was writing in that letter from my disappointment, writing until a clearing came, an affirmation that I write because the process of writing is important to me. It is a wonderful byproduct of that sticking to what's important that my plays have been produced, my poetry well published, and my teaching sought after. Don't you know it, Unsigned, sometimes I receive the grant or commission or position and not my friend.

Somehow you never get around in your short outburst to reporting what I do say after I say I must not listen to the words good and bad as I begin to write. You know, the part about how I seek out response, the long discussion about why working with response is useful to a writer and why reacting to criticism is not.

Well, you probably never went to a writing workshop led by writers instead of critical theorists. You probably never felt free enough inside to invent your own material and work with it no matter how terrifying, no matter how unremunerated.

I do not disdain the critic. I do find the critic counterproductive to starting writing. It is you who is disdaining of our book. It is you who refer to the book as an "allegedly" adult title. Do you think that Christi, who usually writes for children ages 11 to 15, has little to contribute to adults about writing? Certainly you realize that it is adults who are the authors of books for children.

You have done a good job in your short malicious review of attacking us. Well, tearing something apart is quick. It is easy to speak from the scars that have formed over damaged places in one's self rather than offer wisdom from the fire of the wounds below.

Wondering if slasher movies are your favorite,
Poet and Playwright Bender

Christi, when I worked with teachers recently at the Bellevue School District, they said they were using our book in peer writing groups in the classroom. They said the boys and girls were learning how to respond rather than desecrate, how to want to write and share their thoughts rather become laconic or shy or didactic. They said the next generation could have a whole new way of relating to each other.

Writing In A Convertible With The Top Down

Who wants to go to a cocktail party with people who have steel armor for skin and porcupine mantles for hearts?

> Looking forward to the tones
> we help others create,
> Sheila

A KEY: DISCOVER WHERE THE BURR STICKS AND WHY YOU CAN'T JUST BRUSH IT OFF

In our chapter "Cherry Trees" Christi mentions the young adult novel *The Pinballs* by Betsy Byars. This book comes to mind again when we deal with criticism. Thirteen-year-old Harvey has won third prize in an essay contest. The night of the awards dinner, Harvey's father is surprised, not at finding Harvey in his first tie ever, but at finding him in the car at all. His father is rushing off to a poker game and has no time to even drop Harvey off, let alone go to the dinner. Harvey's father pushes Harvey out of the car, throws the gear stick into forward instead of reverse and runs over both of Harvey's legs.

That is what criticism about one's writing can feel like—somebody you expect to come with you, instead runs your legs over on their way to somewhere else and tells you you're in the wrong.

If you take the blame, criticism can indeed cripple you. In order to stay on your feet, you must look not only at the criticism, but at the place it is sticking to your inner self like a tenacious burr that can cause an infection and gut you.

Unsigned managed to hook Christi where she had some self-doubt and Sheila by manipulating her voice. In her letter to Sheila, Christi had a chance to describe that place where the burr stuck. Sheila articulated the distortion in his review.

Christi was able to pull perceptions from the exchange and draft a succinct and pointed letter to *Publisher's Weekly*. She *was* able to defend herself: [handwritten: Why? Who cares?]

January 22, 1992

Dear Ms. Maryles, *Publisher's Weekly*, and your Unsigned Reviewer:

You ran a "My Say" I wrote entitled "The Back Half of the Dog" in your November 29th issue where I describe the invisibility afforded fine children's novels by the adult publishing world. I mention the elitist attitude in this country that claims the adult mind is the only mind worth valuing. And now, just two months later, you prove my point.

My adult nonfiction book *Writing in a Convertible with the Top Down: A Unique Guide for Writers*, co-authored with Sheila Bender, was panned in your January 6th issue: "Most of the authors' condescending advice takes the form of banal letters that sport cheery little closings like 'Yours while the light is long, Sheila' and 'Replanted, looking at a clear blue sky, Christi'—a tone more appropriate to Killien's children's books than this allegedly adult title." There it is. What do my children's books have to do with a review of my adult book other than to imply, in a skewed way, that upbeat, playful adult books are not literary? That they are childlike, hence not valid?

Mr. Unsigned Reviewer takes Sheila's comments about not listening to the internal critic as she begins to write completely out of context. He states that she has a policy of not listening to reader response when in fact the book goes on to demonstrate how a writer can use that response to shape her work. He also offers no examples to back up his claim that the writing process we describe will result in "excruciatingly bad prose." So much for the superior, oh-so-complex adult mind.

The irony of it would be funny if it weren't so tragic. This letter would sound like sour grapes if the review weren't such a slap to children's books and children's book writers in general.

Cheerfully, in spite of
Mr. Unsigned's disdain,
Christi Killien

TAKE IT FOR A SPIN

Our worst fear with this chapter is that readers will think that they don't have to listen to response and learn the revising process. Most drafts are flawed and need revision and rethinking. Having a trusted reader or readers helps a writer work from draft to draft.

But writers can hold out for getting the kind of response that actually helps them write instead of breaking their legs. In "Highway Patrol," Christi and Sheila suggest choosing a partner and writing letters in which you share your responses to each other's words. But what do you do when you get tear-downs instead of responses—from a teacher, in a seminar, from an editor, from family members? How do you handle it?

Write down the words that hurt the most. Where have you heard these words before? Write a paragraph about that.

Visualize yourself addressing the criticizer. Has the criticizer misunderstood? Address his or her misunderstanding in a letter.

Share the criticism and your responses to it with a trusted listener who doesn't have to say a thing. Or put your responses to the criticism in an envelope and mail them to yourself. Just getting your reaction to the criticism out into the world and away from you reduces the sting.

When you send your writing out, you can never tell what the "critics" will say. For instance, an editor who rejected *The Diary of Anne Frank* wrote, "The girl doesn't, it seems to me, have a special perception or feeling which would lift the book above the 'curiosity' level." In 1980, a reviewer for *The Atlantic Monthly*, wrote about the now much-loved Raymond Carver collection of short stories *What We Talk About When We Talk About Love* saying, "There is nothing here to appease a reader's basic literary needs."

When it comes to criticism, all writers always have and always will receive it. Learn what you can from it when it comes your way. You can use your response to the criticism as an opportunity to strengthen your own voice, which when you hear it is universal in its wisdom.

chapter thirteen

Freshman:
What is the writer's job?

SEPTEMBER 26

Dear Sheila,

I saw a bumper sticker yesterday that made me laugh. "I'm lost, but I'm making good time." I thought of when I was in college hating the chemistry and calculus classes that I was taking in my chosen pre-med course, though I was making good time through it all.

In the small English class I was in, I had to write a descriptive essay of a significant person in my life. I enjoyed writing it. I chose Mrs. Robinson, my Sunday School teacher from early high school, an older woman with long gray hair, a woman who loved books and refused to have air-conditioning in her old Houston house. I set my essay in autumn, when the fallen oak leaves around her house would mat the ground.

My English professor gave me a "B" on the paper—not at all an acceptable grade for a pre-med—and wrote "See me" at the top. I met with him and he asked what I was doing in this essay. "I'm describing Mrs. Robinson."

"The grade stands as it is, then," he said, "because you have written a subtext of aging into the description, and if you'd been conscious of it, only then do you deserve an 'A.'"

"The paper is the paper," I argued.

I was not only expected to be able to write the essay, I had to be able to defend it in a way satisfactory to him. Dealing with him was no more fun than the pre-med classes. I changed my major from pre-med to elementary education that semester. I'd get out sooner.

The head trip of people like that professor and Unsigned can really alter one's life, and as I get older I feel again how important it is to know who I am. I knew Mrs. Robinson year round but I chose the images of autumn because I felt they fit the woman. The brittle leaves reminded me of the old pages in her beautiful antique books. That the professor saw a consistent subtext about aging is extra. I gave an accurate description of the woman I knew. Is the writer's job any more than that?

And here's to you,
Mrs. Robinson!
Christi

Writing In A Convertible With The Top Down

October 8

Dear Christi,

I've returned from visiting my son. He is a student at the University of Colorado. His first apartment seems to be a success—from the seven-chili-pepper chili feast he put on with his housemates to the circle of gorgeous young men and women "hacking" in the dining room when the table is pushed aside.

They stand in a circle and keep a small colorful bean-filled sac of stitched suede in the air using the flat surfaces of their feet, their thighs, the bills of their baseball caps, the hollows between their shoulder blades. No hands are allowed, but the soft little sack often dribbles down a chest on its way to the feet. They "dance," and "dig," do "over the rainbow," and "pass." They are good with the moves and the steps. They look like marionettes when their feet come up flat and go back to the floor again between each hit.

They talk and they hack and they talk and they hack—each getting into their moves like a jazz musician in a riff. There is respect there, and patience, and appreciation for the moves.

One morning we hiked in the Rocky Mountain National Park, the aspen leaves clapping in the breeze. Aspens, my son told me, are the largest known organisms in the world because the whole stand is one tree!

Yes, I was thinking as we spotted a hawk screeching to another one on the other side of the trail. Yes. Thumbs up! The world is certainly a go.

Then he told me the philosophy he worked out with a friend when they biked Eldorado Canyon—it's that life is all about "food" and "stuff." If you have the *right* food and the *right* stuff, you don't need anything else.

Christi, this seems to me to speak to our dilemma as creative writers in a left brain analytical culture. A poem, a story, a novel do not reach readers through analysis, but through the images that place the reader in a time and moment. The analytical mind is not where we go to be moved and emotionally informed. If the writing has the right food and the right stuff (layers and layers of leaves in an older woman's yard) it will do its work.

There my son and I stood in our shoes, practicing hacking, the snowcapped Rockies in the background, our packs filled with the goat cheese and sour dough bread we'd bought at an early morning farmer's market. There was nothing else I needed, not even to dream about.

Yours with sun leaking from my skin,

Sheila

OCTOBER 14

Dear Sheila,

I just got back from a day trip to Bellingham and Western Washington University, where I'm setting my new novel, and your letter was in the mail. You talk of Seth's happiness at college in Colorado, and I'm so envious! Walking around Western, I felt, once again, the loneliness I felt at college.

Writing In A Convertible With The Top Down

I'm not saying college was misery for me, not at all. Or not completely. I did well in college, and a part of me thrived. I loved the independence and the focusing down on a goal. But halfway through, and terribly at the end, I was desperate to make a "home." In fact, when I was at Western yesterday, in all its cool, wet, introspective quiet, I must have heard the word "home" more than any other. Was this selective listening? "I have my good bike at home," said one ponytailed man in the Viking Coffee Shop. Another, a blonde woman with a bouncy walk and wide smile, pronounced how glad she was that it was Friday, that she was past some projects now, and that she was "going home!"

I wanted to make a home for myself in college, and was frustrated in doing so. I want to write about that, about a young woman with this same yearning. She wants home. Why does she want it? I ask myself. Why did *I* want it? For now I'll let it suffice that my character is a performer-type person, the oldest child of divorced parents and making her own home is her way of finding out who she is apart from the adaptations she's made in her family. Jenny Walcott is pregnant, just out of high school, and her new boyfriend is not interested in marriage. Her old boyfriend shows up at her doorstep.

Yours with (hopefully) the
right question,
Christi

October 20

Hi Christi,

Rereading your letter at my desk on the second story of my house, I sit under windows and look at the tops of two trees against the storm-grey sky. The just turning Japanese maple (the leaves aren't done on that tree most years until Thanksgiving) thrives at the corner of my house, and the evergreen needles of the tall pine across the street toss in the wind. The motion of the pine tree in every gust reminds me of the aquarium plants my son would buy years ago at the pet store around the corner. It was the first store he could walk to himself, no streets to cross, saved quarters, nickels, dimes, and pennies in his pocket. He'd come home and plunge the tiny leafed things into the water. The air filter bubbled the water through the miniature branches of the plant. Well, that was years ago—at least ten or eleven.

How interesting that the past you are remembering is one of not being yourself, of yearning for a home you could not make. You are going to write yourself a different past in the name of Jenny Walcott who can make herself a home with your sensitive fingers as you build that possibility board by board, so to speak, at your computer.

And here I am, hungry for the past I shared with my children when just a week or so ago I shared the "now" with my son and wanted nothing more! I sit in the present with the past so close I can see the algae on the aquarium walls, smell the outdoors on my son's little boy body as he labors to pin the plant securely in the gravel.

I could not have known how deeply I'd taken in that underwater plant when my son brought it home until I looked *this* day at *this* tree in *this* storm influenced by the longings in your letter.

Today my mother brought me as her guest to a Brandeis fundraising luncheon where three authors spoke—novelist Shawn Wong of Chinese-American descent; magic realism fiction writer Kathleen Alcalá of Hispanic descent; and poet Bernard Harris of African-American descent. They are all writing their way toward home. Mr. Wong wants to claim this country for his own after generations in which his family left a legacy of hurt as well as love. Ms. Alcalá tells the stories of her Latin American grandmother for whom the seen and unseen were not as separate as they are for us further north. Mr. Harris, in what the panel moderator called "social gospel," writes of how his home could have turned out to be the penitentiary instead of the one he shares with his wife and daughter.

Signing the copy of his novel *Homebase*, which I bought, Shawn Wong wrote: "The best stories come from home." But do we remember this home or do we make it? Perhaps in writing we can do both.

Yours where the pine trees and
aquarium plants connect,
Sheila

SHEILA BENDER & CHRISTI KILLIEN GLOVER

A KEY: REMEMBER WHY IT IS IMPORTANT TO YOU TO WRITE

To Christi Mrs. Robinson embodied home. She represented what Christi valued and was missing at college. Mrs. Robinson had children, an almost thirty-year-old car, and an old home in the woods. She was an antique book collector. She found, researched, and often placed them in museums.

In high school, Christi was a librarian with her at the Seaman's Center in the port of Houston. Bookstores tore the front cover and spine off unsold paperbacks to send them back to the publishers and get back return fees because it was a needless expense to send the whole book back. Instead of throwing the faceless books away, the bookstores in Houston would send boxes of them over to the Seaman's Center. Christi and Mrs. Robinson would spend hours with Marksalot pens writing titles across the now naked bindings so the books could be set on shelves where the seaman could see the titles and chose books to take to sea with them. The dried glue and fragments of leftover paper made writing on the spines challenging. But Christi liked doing this project with Mrs. Robinson, who was comfortable with the seaman. Christi learned how to handle herself, too. Mrs. Robinson redirected their flirting; the seaman chose their books, which would be lifelines out of the boredom of long voyages.

After high school, at college, in a new, boxy, air conditioned dorm, Christi didn't feel like who she was. She didn't feel real.

But when she wrote about Mrs. Robinson, she remembered some of herself. In the face of a professor wanting to make that connection "mental," Christi felt helpless.

She didn't know what her job was then. Now she does know—it is not to give a formula for writing or tell why it works. It is to keep making the connections that bring her back to herself.

TAKE IT FOR A SPIN

Read some books in which writer's talk about why they write and what they see as their job. *Writer's on Writing*, edited by George Plimpton, is a set of interviews with writers first published in the *Paris Review*. *The Writer's Journal*, edited by Sheila Bender, is a compilation of unpublished writers' journal entries by forty writers along with commentary on how keeping a journal works for them. Jack Heffron has edited two volumes of *The Best Writing on Writing*. *The Writer on Her Work, Vol 1 and Vol 2*, edited by Janet Sternburg, is also a wonderful collection of writings by writers on writing. This is just a small sampling of the many books that are out there.

Even so, these are voices you probably won't run across in a typical academic education. But they are written by the people for whom writing and being writers comes first. Enjoy their descriptions of where writing comes from and what writers pay attention to. You will find this to be the right "food" and the right "stuff."

chapter fourteen

Garage Sales: Where does the writer discover treasures?

November 1

Dear Sheila,

My neighbor Beth is a "picker"—a middleman for all kinds of garage sale and thrift store stuff that she cleans and repairs and then sells to dealers. Yesterday she called to me as I stood on my deck feeling stuck despite the three feet of novel draft in the corner of my office.

"Did you sell that essay?" she asked.

"Yes!"

The Seattle Review wrote accepting an essay about my grandfather. "I mean, sort of. They'll publish it but all I'll get is two free copies. I want money!"

When we finished *Convertible*, Sheila, I had been selling my children's novels and making money speaking as well. It's been awhile since that *Daffodil* money, though. This new novel is taking its own sweet time. I'm realizing the value of compensation goes beyond money. When I can't impose a deadline on when my novel will be finished and I'm working without remuneration, my sense of self-worth erodes. I don't get paid for the work that's helping me write this novel—literary essays, therapy, and journal writing. And I can't push the novel when it's not jelling.

Before I wrote my first novel, I was a classroom teacher. I used that experience in one way or another through six novels. Maybe I need to get out there to write at all.

"I'm looking for a job," I found myself shouting to Beth.

"You can always junk," she yelled smiling, "It's a wide open field."

And I thought about the value of stuff, the value of our time, of us, of what we do for a living. Maybe *Jenny Walcott* could junk.

Looking for career counseling,
Christi

NOVEMBER 10

Dear Christi,

I read your letter and begin to think of the collectibles I have. My favorite are two *Howdy Doody* sundae spoons.

One year, my father, a pharmaceutical salesman who was gone long hours each week driving his region, took on an extra

Writing In A Convertible With The Top Down

job in December selling socks at Bamberger's Department store in Newark, New Jersey, about ½ hour from our apartment. They were hiring extra help to meet the season's sales demands. My sister and I knew he took the job to afford better Chanukah gifts for us that year. I don't remember what we were given each night when we lit the candles in the Menorah, but I do remember the evening my mother took us to the store by bus to see where my father worked.

He was so happy to see us and it seemed so odd to see my familiar father where only unfamiliar people worked. While he finished his shift, my mother took my sister and me to sit on Santa's lap, to have the new "soft" ice cream they were selling at the store's cafeteria, and we came away with something special—silver-plated *Howdy Doody* sundae spoons. *Howdy Doody* was my favorite TV show. I've saved both those sundae spoons for 37 years now. A lot of the silver plate has come off and ice cream sometimes tastes funny eaten off the spoons because of that, but these two pieces of junk tie me to my family, to a time when my parents were way younger than I am now, to their decision-making, to the holiday season, to the memory of how handsome my father was, to the feeling of being in a family. I see these spoons everyday when I open my silverware drawer.

Have you looked up the word junk yet? Before it came to mean worthless stuff, it meant old metal or paper or glass or rags that were worthless but could be made into something worthwhile. And before that it was the name for ropes made of rushes

149

or hemp, and for mats made of the fibers, and for the fibers themselves pulled apart to stuff and pack boat seams. Then it was the name for hard, salted meat meant for long journeys by boat.

What will Jenny think when she starts finding things older than herself? Things that remind her of a past she did or did not have?

It's off my diet, but I know there's
ice cream in the freezer,
Sheila

December 5

Dear Sheila,

My head is full of job finding strategies. I know virtually zero about marketing myself in the business world, so I'm going to these Career Improvement Group classes. Tuesday was Cover Letter II, and yesterday I spent the day in Phone Skills and Salary Negotiation! This is part of getting out in the world. And I want to for more than the money. For something else I value. Writing is so isolating. I want to be more in the stream of things until my novel unfolds.

And whatever I am doing, I'm still a writer thinking about junk and value. I thought about them again yesterday in Salary Negotiation when the teacher told us to go to a garage sale, barter over a twenty-five cent basket, and feel the tension.

"That tension is what creates opportunity," she said. "Move outside the comfort zone. You're asking people to stretch. If

WRITING IN A CONVERTIBLE WITH THE TOP DOWN

they're comfortable, they won't stretch." There is nothing comfortable to me about haggling over value, especially my own value. Did you know that less than 10% of people try to negotiate their salaries even when given the opportunity? I actually understand this, though. Money is a complex subject, deeply rooted, loaded. So I'm practicing scripts, incorporating the thinking into myself, determining my boundaries. When I actually do it, I imagine it will be like when I actually write. I'll forget all the scripts and do it. But the doing will be informed.

One of the things I love about this career teacher is that she uses child birth metaphors instead of the ubiquitous sports ones.

"Being in the job market is like being pregnant, either you are or you aren't," she once said, and then later, when telling us to trust the process, to let the process support us, she said, "Overcome the need to push. It will birth on its own!"

It amazes me how all this ties into my writing life. Patience. Trusting the process, feeling the tension of opportunity and value at a garage sale, exploring it.

I'm thinking I'd like to do that in a notebook, an ongoing journal about this woman Jenny Walcott as well as about things that interest me that could apply to her. Does she drop out of career school to junk? Doesn't seem to me that junking requires a resume!

Off to haggle over 25 cents,
Christi

151

December 12

Dear Christi,

The late news last night had a feature on a family where the mother birthed twins 95 days apart! That was a record for the time between the births of babies who shared the same womb.

I couldn't help but think that you might get a job and 95 days later have a novel, too! I know that seems impossible—writing a lot while getting used to a new job, but who knows?

I'm proud of you for referencing your writing self as you proceed in the non-exclusive world of "out there." Emily Dickenson says in a poem that we must come at things at a slant. Having career counseling while you invent Jenny's life seems properly, writerly, slant—

Holding my breath for an
excerpt from your notebook,
Sheila

January 3

Dear Sheila,

Here's one where Jenny's talking. The more I listen to her, the more I see she's latched onto a woman who makes her feel she can hack it like I did with Mrs. Robinson at the Houston Seaman's Center:

I went out today with Ann to two estate sales, which were just awful. Junk. Anyway, Charlie and Dorothy and Michael were also there. They let only five of us in at a time, and not

Writing In A Convertible With The Top Down

a minute early. And no numbers! Ann hates poorly run sales. While we were waiting, she told me about a man at one sale who scared her, he was so pushy. This pushy guy who had a ponytail, but wasn't Michael, she said, smiling at Michael who wasn't listening anyway, went into this sale and shouted over her head, "I'll buy that, and that, and that." Ann said she learned that day you don't have to play by the rules.

Ann looked good today, with her red wig and lipstick. She says it's been a tough winter for her, lots of junk and only a few pieces of good jewelry. Most days she wears jean jackets and polyester pants. Her gums bulge over her teeth, puffy but not sore looking. When she smiles it's still nice.

Michael smiled at me. He was standing by the screen door of this tiny house. Michael is short and is either Indian or Mexican, one of the two. I like him. He is the only one of the regulars who doesn't have a store or a mall space. He's into toys like Dorothy. He has two complete Fisher Price McDonalds, but one is missing the Hamburgler. He doesn't know I have a Hamburgler.

He told Ann and Dorothy that he got a beautiful Kitchen Queen for $150.00! He'd been calling this old guy who was going to die every three months. He'd mark his calendar. He called last week and the guy had died. His widow said $500, Michael balked, and her son called out from the background, "Ma, just get rid of it!" So she took $150.00 for something worth a lot more than that. But I guess that's the way this business goes.

Dorothy said some would call us greedy, and that if you ask her that's wrong. "Of course," she said, "there are rotten apples in every barrel, but this work is sacred the way I see it—seeing value in the discarded, the used. Once you see the worth then comes the work of exchange. It's where the rubber meets the road. You look someone in the eye and work them down to what they truly feel something is worth. How is it dishonest to value something that someone else doesn't?"

She's smart and she can teach me a lot. But when I see her I feel sad. I can't help it. How could the Kitchen Queen owner know what anything was worth? As if her husband hadn't just died!

I'm going to ask Ann when I should tell Michael I have the Hamburgler. I wonder what she'll advise me to ask for it.

Liking Jenny a lot,

Christi

A KEY: FIND TREASURES FOR YOUR WRITING

Wherever your life takes you and whatever you find yourself doing or needing to do, no matter how different than writing, there are treasures to take for your writing. A writer's attraction for the idiosyncratic holds in it character and theme. The counselor at the junior high where Christi taught was using subliminal tapes to help herself stop smoking. Christi was fascinated with that and then she saw an article in the newspaper about subliminal tapes and cut it out. When she was writing *Artie's Brief*, subliminal tapes just seemed to fit. Twelve-year-old Artie wanted Gilbert, a foster child, to become more popular and self-confident so he purchased tapes. They were about being calmer and had a title Gilbert wouldn't like. Artie changed the title to something about athletics because he knew Gilbert was interested in being better at sports. In the story, the ploy didn't work, and Artie learns he can't change someone without that person's consciously wanting it. The subliminal tapes were a writer's treasure chest for Christi that held important story pieces—self-knowledge, consciousness, trying to change.

Junking has that same feel to it. What is attractive to Christi the writer about junking as well as subliminal tapes is the tangible qualities. These things work in a story because they are concrete. Here is one way to make sure you are open to gathering such possibilities for your work.

TAKE IT FOR A SPIN

Listen to what people are telling you they are interested in. They might be your instructors, supervisors, friends, mentors, neighbors or strangers on the bus. Look up the terms they use if the terms hook you like Sheila was when she looked up the word "junk" after Christi retrieved it from her neighbor's jaunty conversation.

Write these definitions down in a notebook. Write down who said the words to you and what else they were talking about. Write down where you were when you heard them speaking. When you want to, write a letter to a writing partner or to a friend explaining where you were listening to this word, why you wrote it down, what it means, and what it means to you when you think about it.

You will find yourself enriched and restored as you scribble out these passages. They might find their way into other projects of your writing life, useful though unexpected.

classic books for writers

Bender, Sheila, Ed. *The Writer's Journal: 40 Writers and Their Journals*, Delta, 1996). "Forty very generous writers agreed to share unpublished journal entries and commentary about how they use their writer's journals and how their journal entries influence or become finished work." —Sheila

Campbell, Joseph. *Hero With a Thousand Faces* (Pantheon Books, 2008). "Read it for a sense of how powerful you are." —Christi

Ciardi, John and Williams, Miller. *How Does a Poem Mean?* 2nd Edition (Houghton Mifflin, 1975). "I understood how the lyric in poetry works after reading this book." —Sheila

Elbow, Peter, *Writing With Power, 2nd Edition* (Oxford University Press, 1998). "Elbow's books show us how to get out of being stuck and helpless as writers. *Writing Without Teachers* especially taught me how to put together a writers' group and why they're important." —Sheila

_____. *Writing Without Teachers, 25th Anniversary Edition* (Oxford University Press, 1998). "Useful ideas and argument about how to write without the critic invading and suffocating your writing." —Sheila

Elbow, Peter and Belanoff, Patricia. *A Community of Writers* (McGraw Hill, 1999). "Many of us didn't learn the workshop approach to developing writing while we are in school; here's chance to do that." —Sheila

Field, Syd. Screenplay: *The Foundations of Screenwriting. 6th Edition* (Silman-James Press, 2014). "Syd Field's paradigm and explanations help you make sure you're writing a whole story—not just a great beginning." —Sheila

Files, Meg. *Write From Life: Turning Your Personal Experiences Into Compelling Stories* (Writer's Digest Books, 2002). "Learning how to dig deep is important ." —Sheila

Fiske, Robert Hartwell and Cherry, Laura. *Poem, Revised, 54 Poems, Revisions Discussions* (Marion Street Press, 2008). "A look at the writing processes of 54 modern poets, from complete early drafts through revised versions, including the poets' thoughts on how and way they made changes." —Sheila

Gardner, John. *The Art of Fiction* (Vintage Books, 1991). "This classic is a nitty-gritty discussion from plot to sentence structure." —Christi

Gibbons, Reginald, ed. *The Poet's Work: 29 Masters of 20th Century Poetry on the Origins and Practice of Their Arts* (University of Chicago Press, 1989). "The title of this one tells it all. I really like Karl Shapiro's 'What Is Not Poetry?' and A.D. Hope's 'The Three Faces of Love'" —Sheila

Goldberg, Natalie. *Writing Down the Bone, 2nd Edition* (Shambhala Publications, 2005). "When I'm struck, Natalie's voice—by that I mean her Zen perspective—frees me. I like the way she talks about writing." —Christi

Gornick, Vivian *The Situation and The Story: The Art of Personal Narrative* (Farrar, Straus and Giroux, 2002) "I go to the wisdom in this little book every time I start a blog or essay – 'The situation is the context or circumstance, sometimes the plot; the story is the emotional experience that preoccupies the writer: the insight, the wisdom, the thing one has come to say.'" —Christi

Greenberg, David. *Teaching Poetry to Children* (Continuing Education Publications, 1978). "Here's where I found the like game. There are many fun poetry activities in this little book." —Sheila

Grossman, Florence. *Getting From Here to There: Writing and Reading Poetry* (Boynton/Cook Publishers Inc., 1982). "This book contains fine prompts for beginning poets." —Sheila

Heffron, Jack. *The Writer's Idea Book 10th Anniversary Edition: How to Develop Great Ideas for Fiction, Nonfiction, Poetry, and Screenplays* (Writer's Digest Books, 2012). "Chock full of prompts and ideas to keep you writing." —Sheila

Koch, Kenneth. *Rose, Where Did You Get That Red?: Teaching Great Poetry to Children* (Vintage Reissue Edition, 1990). "Koch's books delightfully combine student and well-known work with ideas for teaching poetry." —Sheila

_____. *I Never Told Anybody: Teaching Writing to Old People* (Teachers and Writers Collaborative, 1997). "Read the author's approach to teaching nursing home residents the art of writing poetry and you will be reminded of its value, of how you, too, can write." —Sheila

_____. *Sleeping on the Wing: Anthology of Modern Poetry With Essays on Reading and Writing* (Vintage, 1982). "A valuable introduction to not only contemporary poetry, but to writing one's own." —Sheila

Kubis, Pat and Howland, Bob. *Writing Fiction, Nonfiction and to Publish* (Longman, 1989). "I like this book for its discussion of plot." —Christi

Limmer, Ruth, ed. *Journey Around My Room: The Autobiography of Louise Bogan* (Viking, 1980). "Since this book is a poet's journal, it helps me see how poetic daily life is." —Sheila

Meredith, Robert C. and Fitzgerald, John D. *Structuring Your Novel: From Basic Idea to Finished Manuscript* (Harper Perennial, 1993). "Incredible cause and effect discussion here—when you're creating a story, everything has to be connected logically." —Christi

Plimpton, George, ed. *Writers at Work, The Paris Review Interviews*, 6th Edition (Viking, 1984). "In this and others of the *Writers at Work* series, you can read the thoughts of many of the great writers." —Sheila

Rainer, Tristine. *The New Diary: How to Use a Journal for Self Guidance and Expanded Creativity* (Distributed by St. Martin's Press, 1978). "I thought we needed a book about journaling here. What's journaling? It's merging feelings, thoughts, dreams, hopes, fears, fantasies, practicalities, worries, facts, and intuitions." —Sheila

Rico, Gabriele Luccer. *Writing the Natural Way Using Right Brain Techniques to Release Your Expressive Powers* (J.P. Tarcher, 2000). 'This is where 'clustering' came from for me." —Sheila

Rilke, Rainer Maria. *Letters to a young Poet* (W.W. Norton, 1993). "Tender advice." —Sheila

Sloane, William. *The Craft of Writing* (W.W. Norton, 1983). "Simple, direct, less philosophical and detailed than John Gardner. If you're trying to find out what good writing is as well as what's bad, he has terrific examples." —Christi

Sparks, Muriel. *Loitering With Intent* (New Directons, Reprint Edition, 2014). "You're reading a novel about a novelist in the act of writing a novel." —Christi

Sternburg, Janet. *The Writer on Her Work, Vol. 1 and 2* (W.W. Norton, 2000). "In Volume I, read the thoughts of Susan

Griffin, Janet Burroway, Michele Murray, Patricia Hampl, Harriet Doerr, Maxine Kumin, and Ursula Le Guin among other writers." —Sheila

Turner, Alberta T., ed. *Fifty Contemporary Poets: The Creative Process* (David McKay Company, 1977). "The first of its kind in which you get to see poets sharing their early versions and their various revisions." —Sheila

Ueland, Brenda. *If You Want to Write: A Book About Art, Independence and Spirit* (BN Publishing, 2010). "I quote this book at young authors' conferences all the time, 'Everybody is talented, original and has something important to say....'" —Christi

Welty, Eudora. *One Writer's Beginnings* (Harvard University Press, 1998). "A beautiful description by a fiction writer of listening, learning to see and finding a voice." —Sheila

notes on the authors

Sheila Bender

Sheila Bender is a poet, author, and writing instructor. She is the founder of Writing It Real, an online community that facilitates writing from personal experience via online classes, editing, coaching, and more. Her publications include a memoir: *A New Theology: Turning to Poetry in a Time of Grief*; poetry: *Behind Us the Way Grows Wider*, and many books on writing. Sheila has served as a Distinguished Lecturer in Seattle University's Creative Writing Program.

She lives in Port Townsend, WA where she teaches regularly for the Centrum Arts Foundation and The Writers' Workshoppe.

Other Books By Sheila Bender

Sorrow's Words: Writing Exericises to Heal Grief
A New Theology: Turning to Poetry in a Time of Grief
Behind Us the Way Grows Wider: Collected Poems 1980-2013
Creative Writing DeMystified
Perfect Phrases for College Application Essays
A Day in the Life: Journaling for Self-Discovery
Writing Personal Poetry: Creating Poems from Your Personal Experience
Keeping a Journal You Love
Writing Personal Essays: How to Shape Your Life Experiences for the Page
The Writer's Journal: 40 Writers and Their Journals

Christi Killien Glover

Christi Killien Glover lived in Seattle, Washington and environs for 35 years, then in April, 2014, she and her husband moved to Puna on the Big Island of Hawaii where they bought an old off-grid hippie house near the ocean on an acre. They're putting in solar and a new catchment tank, nurturing pineapple plants, ducking hurricanes and volcanoes, and hosting family and friends who want to go tropical for a while. She published novels and essays in the old times and now she blogs and writes ebooks.

Praise for Christi Killien's blog Farmlet:

"Your words are strung together like a fine necklace that I can't stop looking at. The light reflecting off of each gem, enhancing the craftsmanship with natural beauty. It's not just how you write, it's what you notice and write about.

—Ross Robinson, Grief Counselor

Other Books by Christi Killien Glover
(under the name Christi Killien)

A Bear Tale (Amazon, Smashwords 2011)
The Daffodils (Scholastic, 1992)
Artie's Brief: The Whole Truth and Nothing But (Houghton Mifflin, Dell, 1989)
Fickle Fever (Houghton Mifflin, Dell, 1988)
Rusty Fertlanger, Lady's Man (Houghton Mifflin, Dell, 1988)
All of the Above (Houghton Mifflin, Dell, 1987)
Putting On An Act (Houghton Mifflin, Dell, 1986)

Made in the USA
Columbia, SC
14 December 2020